101
English
Verbs

The Art of Conjugation

Rory Ryder

Illustrated by Francisco Garnica

New York Chicago San Francisco Lisbon London Madrid Mexico City
Milan New Delhi San Juan Seoul Singapore Sydney Toronto

The **McGraw·Hill** Companies

Library of Congress Cataloging-in-Publication Data

Ryder, Rory.
    101 English verbs : the art of conjugation / Rory Ryder ; Francisco Garnica.
        p.   cm. — (101 verbs)
    Includes index.
    ISBN-10: 0-07-149904-0 (alk. paper)
    ISBN-13: 978-0-07-149904-0
        1. English language—Verb.   2. English language—Textbooks for foreign
speakers.   I. Garnica, Francisco.   II. Title.   III. Title: One hundred and one English
verbs.   IV. Title: One hundred one English verbs.

PE1271.R69   2007
428.2′4—dc22   2007028147

1 2 3 4 5 6 7 8 9 10 11 12 13 14 15 16 17 18 19 20 21 22 23   CTP/CTP   0 9 8 7

ISBN 978-0-07-149904-0
MHID   0-07-149904-0

McGraw-Hill books are available at special quantity discounts to use as premiums and sales promotions, or for use in corporate training programs. For more information, please write to the Director of Special Sales, Professional Publishing, McGraw-Hill, Two Penn Plaza, New York, NY 10121-2298. Or contact your local bookstore.

Also in this series:
101 French Verbs: The Art of Conjugation
101 German Verbs: The Art of Conjugation
101 Italian Verbs: The Art of Conjugation
101 Spanish Verbs: The Art of Conjugation

This book is printed on acid-free paper.

Contents

How to Use This Book

When learning a language, we often have problems remembering the words; it does not mean we have totally forgotten them. It just means that we can't recall them at that particular moment. This book is designed to help learners recall the verbs and their conjugations instantly.

Research

Research has shown that one of the most effective ways to remember something is by association. In this book, the verb (or keyword) has been included in each illustration, which acts as a means to stimulate long-term memory. This method is seven times more effective than passively reading and responding to a list of verbs.

New Approach

Most grammar and verb books relegate the vital task of learning verbs to a black-and-white world of bewildering tables, leaving the student bored and frustrated. *101 English Verbs* is committed to clarifying the importance of this process through stimulating the senses, not by dulling them.

Beautiful Illustrations

The illustrations come together to form a story, an approach beyond conventional verb books. To make the most of this book, spend time with each picture to become familiar with everything that is happening. The pictures construct a story involving characters, plots, and subplots, with clues that add meaning to other pictures. Some pictures are more challenging than others, adding to the fun but, more important, aiding the memory process.

Keywords

We have called the infinitive the "keyword" to refer to its central importance in remembering the multiple ways it can be used. Once you have located the keyword and made the connection with the illustration, you are ready to start to learn the colo(u)r-coded tenses.

Colo(u)r-Coded Verb Tables

The verb tables are designed to save learners valuable time by focusing their attention and allowing them to make immediate connections between the subject and the verb. Making this association clear and simple from the beginning gives learners more confidence to start speaking the language.

This book selects the six most commonly used and useful tenses for beginning learners.

Example Sentences

Each of the 101 conjugation pages contains three sample sentences. These sentences, loosely inspired by the illustration on the page, show the art of conjugation in practice. The verb form in each sentence is colo(u)r coded to help match it up to the tables and to help you understand the correct selection of tense and subject on the grid.

Verb Indexes

The 101 verb conjugations in this book follow a story line, so they are not ordered alphabetically by English infinitive. If you want to look up a specific verb, use the Verb Index to locate the page number. In addition to the 101 verbs featured (which appear in blue), the Verb Index also includes related phrasal verbs (with explanations of their meanings). An additional fifty common irregular English verbs are also listed with their principal parts, allowing the deduction of the required verb form.

Independent Learning

101 English Verbs can be used for self-study, or it can be used as a supplement to a teacher-led course. Pronunciation of all the verbs and their conjugations (spoken by a native speaker) are available online at **www.learnverbs.com**.

Master the Verbs

Once you are confident with each tense, congratulate yourself because you have learned more than 3,600 verb forms—an achievement that can otherwise take a long time to master!

Meet the Characters

Hello, I'm (*contraction* = I am) Pete.

I'm 22 years old. I'm a part-time student, and I have a couple of odd jobs. I like painting and constructing things. One of these days, I will make a famous invention!

My girlfriend is called Marie. She likes to have fun and to party. She is the most beautiful girl in the world!

Woof! Woof! I am Toby!

I am the only blue dog in the world. I like to run and to chase cats and cars! But I live on my own, and I want a friendly owner.

Hi, my name is Marie. I don't want to tell you my age—it's a secret! I am a fashion designer. I love animals, but I don't have a pet. I like to walk on the beach, to play, and to swim.

I have a boyfriend, Pete, who is kind and funny, and he likes to cook!

Hello, I'm Max. I'm a successful director. I like to collect things. My favo(u)rite place in the world is Las Vegas!

The Art of Conjugation

The art of conjugation is the ability to select the correct verb form. Using this book, this skill is as simple as locating a square on a grid. Simply follow these steps:

- Select the correct verb (use the Verb Index at the back of the book to find the appropriate page).
- Select the correct person (see the list of personal pronouns in the next section to help you choose the correct row).
- Select the correct tense (see the explanations on pages x–xvii to guide you to choose the correct column).

Select the correct tense

↓

Sub.	Present Simple Present Cont.	Past Continuous	Past Simple	Future	Conditional	Present Perfect
I	paint — am painting	was painting	painted	will paint	would paint	have painted
You	paint — are painting	were painting	painted	will paint	would paint	have painted
He She It	paints — is painting	was painting	painted	will paint	would paint	has painted
We	paint — are painting	were painting	painted	will paint	would paint	have painted
You (pl)	paint — are painting	were painting	painted	will paint	would paint	have painted
They	paint — are painting	were painting	painted	will paint	would paint	have painted

Select the correct person

. . . to locate the correct verb form!

The Person of the Verb

To select the correct person, you must know the subject of the verb: who is doing the action. In each conjugation panel, there are six rows. Each row corresponds to a *person*, represented in the first column by the following personal pronouns.

Personal Pronouns

I	the speaker
You	singular: formal and informal
He She It	male person female person neuter thing
We	plural: includes the speaker
You (pl)	plural: formal and informal
They	plural: any gender

Note the following:

- Pronouns can be grouped by person:

  first person: *I*, *we* (includes the speaker or writer)
  second person: *you* (the person or persons being addressed)
  third person: *he*, *she*, *it*, *they* (the person or persons talked about). The third person is also used for nouns or names of people or animals that are subjects of the sentence.

- Pronouns can also be grouped by number:

  singular: *I*, *you*, *he*, *she*, *it* (one single person, animal, or object)
  plural: *we*, *you*, *they* (more than one person, animal, or object)

- The only subject pronouns that indicate gender are those for third person singular: *he* (masculine), *she* (feminine), and *it* (neuter, no gender).

Verb Tenses

As well as knowing the appropriate verb name (the keyword or infinitive) and the correct person, you also need to select the correct tense. Tenses relate to time: when the action or state takes place. And while there are three basic time states (past, present, and future), there are at least fourteen different tenses in English! But don't worry—many are not frequently used, and this book has selected only six of the most common tenses that you will need. All six tenses are colo(u)r-coded, to help you recognize and learn them. The following pages explain each tense and when it is used. They also indicate how each tense is formed.

Present Simple

Also known as: Present

The present simple tense of regular verbs consists of the basic verb form (the infinitive without the word **to**) in all persons, except for the third person singular. This form (he, she, it) adds **-s** (or **-es** if the verb ends in **-ch, -s, -sh, -x**, and **-z**; **-ses** if the verb ends in **-s**; while a final **-y** is replaced with **-ies**).

Present Simple			
	I	cook	-
	You	cook	-
	He/She/It	cook	s
	We	cook	-
	You	cook	-
	They	cook	-

The present simple tense is used in English in the following situations:

- for habitual actions that happen regularly (but are not necessarily happening now):

   Toby brings me the newspaper in the morning.

- for descriptions of ongoing states and permanent characteristics:

   I am what I am—a man with many faults.

- for the subordinate clause of a present/future conditional sentence:

   If you organize your things, you'll find them more easily.

Note the following forms:

- for questions and intensives, use do (does for third person singular) plus the basic verb form:

Do you like to swim in the sea? When do you swim in the pool?

I do like the pool.

- for negatives, use do not/don't (does not/doesn't for third person singular) plus the basic verb form:

  I don't like the sea.   **And he doesn't like the pool.**

Present Continuous

Also known as: Present progressive

The present continuous tense of regular verbs is formed with the present simple tense of **to be** plus the present participle. The present participle is formed by adding **-ing** to the basic verb form (removing any final **-e**).

Present Continuous	I	am	cook	ing
	You	are	cook	ing
	He/She/It	is	cook	ing
	We	are	cook	ing
	You	are	cook	ing
	They	are	cook	ing

Forms of the present continuous are commonly contracted: I'm cooking (I am cooking); you're cooking (you are cooking); and similarly with he's/she's/it's/we're/they're cooking.

The present continuous tense is used for actions going on at the current time:

Toby is growing bigger every day.

The different use of the present simple (for habitual actions) and the present continuous (for current actions) is illustrated in this example:

I normally drink coffee in the morning, but today I am drinking fruit juice.

Note the following forms:

- for questions, invert the subject pronoun and the **to be** part of the verb:

  Are you swimming in the sea? Why are you swimming in the sea?

- for intensives, add stress to the **to be** part of the verb; for negatives, insert *not* before the present participle:

  I *am* swimming in the sea! I'm *not* swimming in the pool.

Past Continuous

Also known as: Past progressive

The past continuous is formed by adding the past simple form of **to be** (*was/were*) plus the present participle. The present participle is formed by adding *-ing* to the basic verb form (removing any final *-e*).

Past Continuous	I	was	cook	ing
	You	were	cook	ing
	He/She/It	was	cook	ing
	We	were	cook	ing
	You	were	cook	ing
	They	were	cook	ing

The past continuous tense is used in English in the following situations:

- for describing actions that proceeded in the past:

  Max was playing cards all last night.

- for describing actions that were ongoing when something else happened:

  Pete was swimming in the sea when a school of dolphins swam up.

- for describing background actions such as time and weather:

  It was raining as Marie and Toby sat on the beach.

For habitual or repeated actions in the past, use the auxiliary *used to* or *would* plus the base verb form:

  I *used to* swim in the sea.

  Last summer I *would* swim all day in the sea.

Note the following forms:

- for questions, invert the subject pronoun and the **to be** part of the verb:

  Were you swimming in the sea?

- for intensives, add stress to the **to be** part of the verb; for negatives, insert *not* before the present participle:

  I *was* swimming in the sea! I was *not* swimming in the pool.

Past Simple

Also known as: Past

The past simple tense of regular verbs is formed by adding **-ed** to the base form of the verb. (Verbs ending in **-e** just add **-d**; verbs ending in **-y** replace it with **-ied**.) See the Verb Index for common irregular past simple verb forms. The form is the same for all persons (except **to be**: *was/were*).

Past Simple			
	I	cook	ed
	You	cook	ed
	He/She/It	cook	ed
	We	cook	ed
	You	cook	ed
	They	cook	ed

The past simple tense is used in English in the following situations:

- for single actions that happened in the past:

  Max put all his money on the table.

- for completed actions in the past that were part of a sequence:

  He entered through the window, stole some valuables, and then left.

- for describing an action that occurs while another action (in the imperfect) was taking place:

  Pete was swimming in the sea when a school of dolphins swam up.

Note the following forms:

- for questions and intensives, use did (past simple of **to do**) plus basic verb form:

  Did you like to swim in the sea last summer? When did you swim in the pool?

  I did like the pool.

- for negatives, use did not (contracted to didn't) plus basic verb form:

  I didn't like the sea.

Future

Also known as: Simple future

The future is formed from the future form of **to be** (*will*, or its contraction *'ll*) and the basic verb form. It is the same for all persons, and there are no irregularities.

Future	I	will	cook
	You	will	cook
	He/She/It	will	cook
	We	will	cook
	You	will	cook
	They	will	cook

The future is used in English in the following situations:

- for describing actions that will happen at some future time:

  Tomorrow I will write some e-mails.

- for describing immediately intended actions or imminent events:

  And now I will show you my invention!

- for describing the consequences of a present/future conditional sentence:

  If you sign here, sir, you will receive this letter.

- for expressing an order (instead of using a command):

  Students, will you please study for the exams!

Note: the verb **to be going** plus the infinitive is used to express future intention:

Now I'm going to take you for a flight in the time machine.

Note the following forms:

- for questions, invert the subject pronoun and the **to be** part of the verb:

  Will you swim in the sea?

- for intensives, add stress to the **to be** part of the verb; for negatives, insert *not* before the present participle (*will not* can contract to *won't*):

  I will swim in the sea! I will not swim in the pool.

Conditional

Also described as a modal auxiliary **would**.
The conditional is formed from **would** and the base verb form.

Conditional			
	I	would	cook
	You	would	cook
	He/She/It	would	cook
	We	would	cook
	You	would	cook
	They	would	cook

The conditional is used in English in the following situations:

- for describing conditional situations that might have happened (but did not):

  If I had a box of matches, I would light this fire easily.

- for asking a question about a hypothetical or possible scenario:

  Would you scream in her situation?

- for softening a demand or wish:

  Would you read aloud that dish, please? I can't pronounce it.

Note the following forms:

- for questions, invert the subject pronoun and the **to be** part of the verb:

  Would you swim in the sea, if you saw sharks?

- for intensives, add stress to the **would** part of the verb; for negatives, insert *not* before the present participle (**would not** can contract to **wouldn't**):

  I *would* swim in the sea! I would *not* swim in the pool.

Present Perfect

Also known as: Perfect or present perfective

The present perfect tense is formed by combining the present simple form of **to have** plus the past participle. The past participle of regular verbs is formed by adding **-ed** to the basic verb form (add just **-d** to verbs ending in **-e**).

Present Perfect				
	I	have	cook	ed
	You	have	cook	ed
	He/She/It	has	cook	ed
	We	have	cook	ed
	You	have	cook	ed
	They	have	cook	ed

The present perfect tense is used in English for past actions that relate to the present:

> I **have directed** lots of movie stars in my career.

(His career is not over yet.)

> Max **has** always **wanted** to collect furniture.

(He has wanted to do this for some time; he still does want to.)

Note the following forms:

- for questions, invert the subject pronoun and the **to be** part of the verb:

> **Have** you **swum** in the sea yet?

- for intensives, add stress to the **to have** part of the verb; for negatives, insert **not** before the present participle (**have not** can contract to **haven't**):

> I **have swum** in the sea! But I **have n't swum** in the pool.

Command

Also known as: Imperative

The command form is shown in red type on each conjugation page. It is the same form as the second person present simple tense (without the **you**), so the singular and plural forms are the same. The first person plural command is formed by adding **Let's** (= **Let us**).

Let's go to the future, Pete! But don't go over the top!

The command is used for telling someone to do something, as an order, request, or demand:

Students, read this book! It will help you learn English verbs!

Sit down! Relax! Take the weight off your feet!

Finish the race as fast as you can!

The negative form of the command (for telling someone *not* to do something) is formed by adding do not (contracted to don't) to the active command:

Don't go down there, Max! You'll regret it!

The command can be softened by adding *please* or using the conditional:

Pete, please repair our vehicle! I don't want to be stuck here forever.

Another way to make a command is to use the future tense:

Students, will you please study for the exams!

Gerund

Also known as: Verbal noun

The gerund is shown opposite the infinitive on each conjugation page. It is formed by adding **-ing** to the verb stem (removing any final **-e**); it is the present participle used as a noun.

The gerund is used in English to describe the action of the verb (often interchangeable with the infinitive):

Polishing is very hard work!

I love dancing; it keeps me fit and healthy.

Reflexive Verbs

Some English verbs refer back to the subject, like the English verb *to wash oneself* (*I wash myself, you wash yourself*, and so on). These verbs include the reflexive pronoun.

Reflexive Pronouns

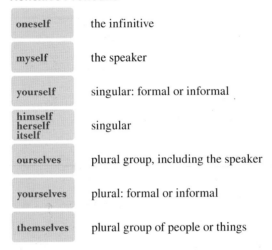

oneself	the infinitive
myself	the speaker
yourself	singular: formal or informal
himself herself itself	singular
ourselves	plural group, including the speaker
yourselves	plural: formal or informal
themselves	plural group of people or things

Here are a few examples:

He **was kicking** *himself* for being so stupid.

"Clean up after *yourself*!" she would shout.

I think that we **have found** *ourselves* a pet!

Phrasal Verbs

Phrasal verbs are a common feature of English. They consist of a main verb plus another word or words, usually prepositions. The following conjugated verbs are phrasal verbs:

#19 to go down   #24 to wake up
#20 to sit down   #28 to go out

Common prepositions used in phrasal verbs include: *around, back, by, down, for, in, on, out, over, through, under, up,* and *with.* A phrasal verb is often idiomatic; that is, its meaning cannot be guessed from the combined meanings of each individual word in the phrase.

The Verb Index contains common phrasal verb forms of the 101 verbs contained in this book. Several are illustrated in the example sentences; their meanings are explained in parentheses.

We need to talk through our disagreement, Marie! (= *To resolve*)

This situation calls for your help, Toby! (= *Requires*)

Marie's face lit up when the fire began to blaze. (= *Brightened with pleasure*)

That's why their plans fell through. (= *Did not take place as intended*)

After all that work, he polished off a whole steak. (= *Ate entirely*)

I will not put up with any more losses. (= *Will not accept*)

I will find out what he likes to eat. (= *Discover*)

Pete has come up with a great idea. (= *Has thought of*)

The Passive

The passive construction is commonly used in English. In passive sentences, the subject is acted upon; that is, the action happens to the subject.

The passive is formed by the appropriate tense of the verb **to be** plus the past participle. The passive infinitive is shown in olive text beneath the infinitive in each conjugation. See the inside back cover for a model conjugation.

These examples show the passive forms of the infinitive and each tense:

I love to be kissed! Please don't stop!

Are the files organized alphabetically?

Meanwhile, Pete and Marie's house was being entered by Nico!

The food was cooked at 300 degrees.

What subject will be learned/learnt at school today?

If I had a box of matches, this fire would be lit easily.

All of Max's clothes have been lost!

If the agent (who performs the action) is mentioned, it usually follows **by**.

This restaurant is liked by all its visitors.

Sub.	Present Simple Present Cont.	Past Continuous	Past Simple	Future	Conditional	Present Perfect
I	direct – am directing	was directing	directed	will direct	would direct	have directed
You	direct – are directing	were directing	directed	will direct	would direct	have directed
He She It	directs – is directing	was directing	directed	will direct	would direct	has directed
We	direct – are directing	were directing	directed	will direct	would direct	have directed
You (pl)	direct – are directing	were directing	directed	will direct	would direct	have directed
They	direct – are directing	were directing	directed	will direct	would direct	have directed

Max **is directing** a movie about English verbs.

I **have directed** lots of movie stars in my career.

As I am very busy, I **will** now **direct** you to the exit! (= *I will point you toward the exit.*)

1

Sub.	Present Simple Present Cont.	Past Continuous	Past Simple	Future	Conditional	Present Perfect
I	have — am having	was having	had	will have	would have	have had
You	have — are having	were having	had	will have	would have	have had
He She It	has — is having	was having	had	will have	would have	has had
We	have — are having	were having	had	will have	would have	have had
You (pl)	have — are having	were having	had	will have	would have	have had
They	have — are having	were having	had	will have	would have	have had

Nico has a green suitcase and a handkerchief.

Max looks important because he has a suit on. (= *He is wearing a suit.*)

Max has told Nico to get off his chair. Nico has had a bad day!

Note: many forms are commonly contracted: I've (I have), you've (you have), he's (he has), she's (she has), it's (it has), we've (we have), they've (they have).

2

Sub.	Present Simple Present Cont.	Past Continuous	Past Simple	Future	Conditional	Present Perfect
I	want – am wanting	was wanting	wanted	will want	would want	have wanted
You	want – are wanting	were wanting	wanted	will want	would want	have wanted
He She It	wants – is wanting	was wanting	wanted	will want	would want	has wanted
We	want – are wanting	were wanting	wanted	will want	would want	have wanted
You (pl)	want – are wanting	were wanting	wanted	will want	would want	have wanted
They	want – are wanting	were wanting	wanted	will want	would want	have wanted

Max has always wanted to collect furniture.

I want to buy six more chairs.

Max is so rich, he wants for nothing. (= *He lacks nothing.*)

3

to be able (to)

no passive

Sub.	Present Simple Present Cont.	Past Continuous	Past Simple	Future	Conditional	Present Perfect
I	am able to (can) – x	was able to	could	will be able to	would be able to (could)	have been able to
You	are able to (can) – x	were able to	could	will be able to	would be able to (could)	have been able to
He She It	is able to (can) – x	was able to	could	will be able to	would be able to (could)	has been able to
We	are able to (can) – x	were able to	could	will be able to	would be able to (could)	have been able to
You (pl)	are able to (can) – x	were able to	could	will be able to	would be able to (could)	have been able to
They	are able to (can) – x	were able to	could	will be able to	would be able to (could)	have been able to

Will you **be able** to buy that beautiful chair?

I am so rich that I **can** buy ten of them.

Then **would** you **be able** to spare me some money?

4

Sub.	Present Simple Present Cont.	Past Continuous	Past Simple	Future	Conditional	Present Perfect
I	create – am creating	was creating	created	will create	would create	have created
You	create – are creating	were creating	created	will create	would create	have created
He She It	creates – is creating	was creating	created	will create	would create	has created
We	create – are creating	were creating	created	will create	would create	have created
You (pl)	create – are creating	were creating	created	will create	would create	have created
They	create – are creating	were creating	created	will create	would create	have created

Today I **am creating** man and woman.

Yesterday I **created** day and night.

The naughty angels **have created** an unholy mess.

to be painted   paint!

Sub.	Present Simple Present Cont.	Past Continuous	Past Simple	Future	Conditional	Present Perfect
I	paint – am painting	was painting	painted	will paint	would paint	have painted
You	paint – are painting	were painting	painted	will paint	would paint	have painted
He She It	paints – is painting	was painting	painted	will paint	would paint	has painted
We	paint – are painting	were painting	painted	will paint	would paint	have painted
You (pl)	paint – are painting	were painting	painted	will paint	would paint	have painted
They	paint – are painting	were painting	painted	will paint	would paint	have painted

I am an artist: I paint pictures.

I wish you would paint like Picasso, Pete!

Last night Pete painted the town red. (= *Pete celebrated. idiomatic*)

Sub.	Present Simple Present Cont.	Past Continuous	Past Simple	Future	Conditional	Present Perfect
I	dance – am dancing	was dancing	danced	will dance	would dance	have danced
You	dance – are dancing	were dancing	danced	will dance	would dance	have danced
He She It	dances – is dancing	was dancing	danced	will dance	would dance	has danced
We	dance – are dancing	were dancing	danced	will dance	would dance	have danced
You (pl)	dance – are dancing	were dancing	danced	will dance	would dance	have danced
They	dance – are dancing	were dancing	danced	will dance	would dance	have danced

When Marie dances, she moves her arms and legs energetically.

Wow, you were dancing very well, Marie!

I love dancing; it keeps me fit and healthy.

to read
to be read

Sub.	Present Simple / Present Cont.	Past Continuous	Past Simple	Future	Conditional	Present Perfect
I	read – am reading	was reading	read	will read	would read	have read
You	read – are reading	were reading	read	will read	would read	have read
He She It	reads – is reading	was reading	read	will read	would read	has read
We	read – are reading	were reading	read	will read	would read	have read
You (pl)	read – are reading	were reading	read	will read	would read	have read
They	read – are reading	were reading	read	will read	would read	have read

Pete and Marie are reading the menu in a restaurant.

Would you read aloud that dish, please? I can't pronounce it. (= *Would you read the name of that dish aloud?*)

Students, read this book! It will help you learn English verbs!

8

Sub.	Present Simple Present Cont.	Past Continuous	Past Simple	Future	Conditional	Present Perfect
I	quit – am quitting	was quitting	quitted	will quit	would quit	have quitted
You	quit – are quitting	were quitting	quitted	will quit	would quit	have quitted
He She It	quits – is quitting	was quitting	quitted	will quit	would quit	has quitted
We	quit – are quitting	were quitting	quitted	will quit	would quit	have quitted
You (pl)	quit – are quitting	were quitting	quitted	will quit	would quit	have quitted
They	quit – are quitting	were quitting	quitted	will quit	would quit	have quitted

We **will** both **quit** smoking—it's a bad habit.

I thought you two **quitted** smoking last month!

Quit reminding us of our failure to quit!

9

to find
to be found

Sub.	Present Simple Present Cont.	Past Continuous	Past Simple	Future	Conditional	Present Perfect
I	find — am finding	was finding	found	will find	would find	have found
You	find — are finding	were finding	found	will find	would find	have found
He She It	finds — is finding	was finding	found	will find	would find	has found
We	find — are finding	were finding	found	will find	would find	have found
You (pl)	find — are finding	were finding	found	will find	would find	have found
They	find — are finding	were finding	found	will find	would find	have found

Pete, look what I found in that box—a dog!

I think that we have found ourselves a pet! Let's call him Toby.

I will find out what he likes to eat. (= *I will discover.*)

10

Sub.	Present Simple / Present Cont.	Past Continuous	Past Simple	Future	Conditional	Present Perfect
I	grow – am growing	was growing	grew	will grow	would grow	have grown
You	grow – are growing	were growing	grew	will grow	would grow	have grown
He She It	grows – is growing	was growing	grew	will grow	would grow	has grown
We	grow – are growing	were growing	grew	will grow	would grow	have grown
You (pl)	grow – are growing	were growing	grew	will grow	would grow	have grown
They	grow – are growing	were growing	grew	will grow	would grow	have grown

Toby **is growing** bigger every day.

Toby, you **will grow** as big as this tree!

Owning a dog **has grown** on me. (= *Owning a dog has become more appealing.*)

11

to be brought

Sub.	Present Simple Present Cont.	Past Continuous	Past Simple	Future	Conditional	Present Perfect
I	bring – am bringing	was bringing	brought	will bring	would bring	have brought
You	bring – are bringing	were bringing	brought	will bring	would bring	have brought
He She It	brings – is bringing	was bringing	brought	will bring	would bring	has brought
We	bring – are bringing	were bringing	brought	will bring	would bring	have brought
You (pl)	bring – are bringing	were bringing	brought	will bring	would bring	have brought
They	bring – are bringing	were bringing	brought	will bring	would bring	have brought

Toby brings me the newspaper in the morning.

Yesterday he brought me slippers instead—very funny!

I hope my newspaper will be brought to me tomorrow.

cooking
cook!

to cook
to be cooked

Sub.	Present Simple Present Cont.	Past Continuous	Past Simple	Future	Conditional	Present Perfect
I	cook – am cooking	was cooking	cooked	will cook	would cook	have cooked
You	cook – are cooking	were cooking	cooked	will cook	would cook	have cooked
He She It	cooks – is cooking	was cooking	cooked	will cook	would cook	has cooked
We	cook – are cooking	were cooking	cooked	will cook	would cook	have cooked
You (pl)	cook – are cooking	were cooking	cooked	will cook	would cook	have cooked
They	cook – are cooking	were cooking	cooked	will cook	would cook	have cooked

Yesterday, as usual, we **were cooking** dinner together in the kitchen.

You **cook** better than my mother, Pete!

The dinner **was cooked** at 300 degrees.

13

to like

liking

to be liked

like!

Sub.	Present Simple / Present Cont.	Past Continuous	Past Simple	Future	Conditional	Present Perfect
I	like — am liking	was liking	liked	will like	would like	have liked
You	like — are liking	were liking	liked	will like	would like	have liked
He She It	likes — is liking	was liking	liked	will like	would like	has liked
We	like — are liking	were liking	liked	will like	would like	have liked
You (pl)	like — are liking	were liking	liked	will like	would like	have liked
They	like — are liking	were liking	liked	will like	would like	have liked

I really **liked** that meal.

You **will like** the dessert even more!

This restaurant is liked by all its visitors.

14

Sub.	Present Simple Present Cont.	Past Continuous	Past Simple	Future	Conditional	Present Perfect
I	open – am opening	was opening	opened	will open	would open	have opened
You	open – are opening	were opening	opened	will open	would open	have opened
He She It	opens – is opening	was opening	opened	will open	would open	has opened
We	open – are opening	were opening	opened	will open	would open	have opened
You (pl)	open – are opening	were opening	opened	will open	would open	have opened
They	open – are opening	were opening	opened	will open	would open	have opened

I wish this bottle **would open**!

Pete, why **are** you **opening** that bottle without a bottle opener?

Oww, my teeth! When **will** the hospital **open**?

to drink
to be drunk

Sub.	Present Simple Present Cont.	Past Continuous	Past Simple	Future	Conditional	Present Perfect
I	drink – am drinking	was drinking	drank	will drink	would drink	have drunk
You	drink – are drinking	were drinking	drank	will drink	would drink	have drunk
He She It	drinks – is drinking	was drinking	drank	will drink	would drink	has drunk
We	drink – are drinking	were drinking	drank	will drink	would drink	have drunk
You (pl)	drink – are drinking	were drinking	drank	will drink	would drink	have drunk
They	drink – are drinking	were drinking	drank	will drink	would drink	have drunk

I normally **drink** coffee in the morning, but today I **am drinking** fruit juice.

What **were** you **drinking** yesterday evening?

Toby was obviously thirsty: he **drank** <u>up</u> all the water. (= *He finished all the water.*)

16

Sub.	Present Simple Present Cont.	Past Continuous	Past Simple	Future	Conditional	Present Perfect
I	sing – am singing	was singing	sang	will sing	would sing	have sung
You	sing – are singing	were singing	sang	will sing	would sing	have sung
He She It	sings – is singing	was singing	sang	will sing	would sing	has sung
We	sing – are singing	were singing	sang	will sing	would sing	have sung
You (pl)	sing – are singing	were singing	sang	will sing	would sing	have sung
They	sing – are singing	were singing	sang	will sing	would sing	have sung

Pete, what song are you singing?

That song was sung much better by Elvis Presley.

Next year I'll sing on TV, and I'll win the "Idol" competition—you'll see!

to sleep sleeping
to be slept sleep!

Sub.	Present Simple Present Cont.	Past Continuous	Past Simple	Future	Conditional	Present Perfect
I	sleep – am sleeping	was sleeping	slept	will sleep	would sleep	have slept
You	sleep – are sleeping	were sleeping	slept	will sleep	would sleep	have slept
He She It	sleeps – is sleeping	was sleeping	slept	will sleep	would sleep	has slept
We	sleep – are sleeping	were sleeping	slept	will sleep	would sleep	have slept
You (pl)	sleep – are sleeping	were sleeping	slept	will sleep	would sleep	have slept
They	sleep – are sleeping	were sleeping	slept	will sleep	would sleep	have slept

Marie **sleeps** in a large bed.

You **slept** until midday! You must have been exhausted.

Do you think you **would sleep** through a hurricane? (= *Would you stay asleep for the duration of a hurricane?*)

going down
go down!

to go down
to be gone down

Sub.	Present Simple Present Cont.	Past Continuous	Past Simple	Future	Conditional	Present Perfect
I	go down – am going down	was going down	went down	will go down	would go down	have gone down
You	go down – are going down	were going down	went down	will go down	would go down	have gone down
He She It	goes down – is going down	was going down	went down	will go down	would go down	has gone down
We	go down – are going down	were going down	went down	will go down	would go down	have gone down
You (pl)	go down – are going down	were going down	went down	will go down	would go down	have gone down
They	go down – are going down	were going down	went down	will go down	would go down	have gone down

Those stairs **go down** to the basement.

Max **went down** the stairs to the club.

Don't go down there, Max! You'll regret it!

19

to sit down

to be sat down

Sub.	Present Simple / Present Cont.	Past Continuous	Past Simple	Future	Conditional	Present Perfect
I	sit down / am sitting down	was sitting down	sat down	will sit down	would sit down	have sat down
You	sit down / are sitting down	were sitting down	sat down	will sit down	would sit down	have sat down
He She It	sits down / is sitting down	was sitting down	sat down	will sit down	would sit down	has sat down
We	sit down / are sitting down	were sitting down	sat down	will sit down	would sit down	have sat down
You (pl)	sit down / are sitting down	were sitting down	sat down	will sit down	would sit down	have sat down
They	sit down / are sitting down	were sitting down	sat down	will sit down	would sit down	have sat down

Max **was sitting down** on his chair.

Sit down! Relax! Take the weight off your feet!

When Max **sits down**, he always falls asleep.

20

Sub.	Present Simple Present Cont.	Past Continuous	Past Simple	Future	Conditional	Present Perfect
I	play – am playing	was playing	played	will play	would play	have played
You	play – are playing	were playing	played	will play	would play	have played
He She It	plays – is playing	was playing	played	will play	would play	has played
We	play – are playing	were playing	played	will play	would play	have played
You (pl)	play – are playing	were playing	played	will play	would play	have played
They	play – are playing	were playing	played	will play	would play	have played

Max **was playing** cards all last night.

Card **playing** and pool are very popular activities in this club.

Max **played** up his winnings and **played** down his losses. (= *Max exaggerated his winnings and diminished the importance of his losses.*)

21

to put

to be put

Sub.	Present Simple Present Cont.	Past Continuous	Past Simple	Future	Conditional	Present Perfect
I	put – am putting	was putting	put	will put	would put	have put
You	put – are putting	were putting	put	will put	would put	have put
He She It	puts – is putting	was putting	put	will put	would put	has put
We	put – are putting	were putting	put	will put	would put	have put
You (pl)	put – are putting	were putting	put	will put	would put	have put
They	put – are putting	were putting	put	will put	would put	have put

Max **put** all his tokens on the table.

I **will** not **put** up with any more losses! (= *I will not accept losing any more.*)

Are you **putting** all your eggs in one basket? (= *Are you risking everything on one outcome? idiomatic*)

Sub.	Present Simple Present Cont.	Past Continuous	Past Simple	Future	Conditional	Present Perfect
I	lose — am losing	was losing	lost	will lose	would lose	have lost
You	lose — are losing	were losing	lost	will lose	would lose	have lost
He She It	loses — is losing	was losing	lost	will lose	would lose	has lost
We	lose — are losing	were losing	lost	will lose	would lose	have lost
You (pl)	lose — are losing	were losing	lost	will lose	would lose	have lost
They	lose — are losing	were losing	lost	will lose	would lose	have lost

Too bad! All of Max's clothes have been lost!

If you play for high stakes, you will lose your possessions.

The funny side of things was lost on Max. (= *Max could not appreciate the comic aspect of the situation.*)

23

to wake up

to be woken up

Sub.	Present Simple Present Cont.	Past Continuous	Past Simple	Future	Conditional	Present Perfect
I	wake up am waking up	was waking up	woke up	will wake up	would wake up	have woken up
You	wake up are waking up	were waking up	woke up	will wake up	would wake up	have woken up
He She It	wakes up is waking up	was waking up	woke up	will wake up	would wake up	has woken up
We	wake up are waking up	were waking up	woke up	will wake up	would wake up	have woken up
You (pl)	wake up are waking up	were waking up	woke up	will wake up	would wake up	have woken up
They	wake up are waking up	were waking up	woke up	will wake up	would wake up	have woken up

Marie usually **wakes up** early.

This morning she was woken up by the alarm clock.

Wake up and smell the coffee! (= *Become aware of what is going on around you.*
   idiomatic)

24

Sub.	Present Simple Present Cont.	Past Continuous	Past Simple	Future	Conditional	Present Perfect
I	run – am running	was running	ran	will run	would run	have run
You	run – are running	were running	ran	will run	would run	have run
He She It	runs – is running	was running	ran	will run	would run	has run
We	run – are running	were running	ran	will run	would run	have run
You (pl)	run – are running	were running	ran	will run	would run	have run
They	run – are running	were running	ran	will run	would run	have run

Marie and Pete were running along the street.

Would you run without looking where you are going?

Pete, you are running the risk of an accident. Don't run over any children! (= *You are taking the chance of an accident. [idiomatic]; Don't knock down any children.*)

to fall

no passive

Sub.	Present Simple Present Cont.	Past Continuous	Past Simple	Future	Conditional	Present Perfect
I	fall — am falling	was falling	fell	will fall	would fall	have fallen
You	fall — are falling	were falling	fell	will fall	would fall	have fallen
He She It	falls — is falling	was falling	fell	will fall	would fall	has fallen
We	fall — are falling	were falling	fell	will fall	would fall	have fallen
You (pl)	fall — are falling	were falling	fell	will fall	would fall	have fallen
They	fall — are falling	were falling	fell	will fall	would fall	have fallen

Pete is falling into the hole. Help!

It's the first time I have ever fallen down a drain!

That's why their plans for the day fell through. (= *Their plans did not happen as intended.*)

26

Sub.	Present Simple Present Cont.	Past Continuous	Past Simple	Future	Conditional	Present Perfect
I	search – am searching	was searching	searched	will search	would search	have searched
You	search – are searching	were searching	searched	will search	would search	have searched
He She It	searches – is searching	was searching	searched	will search	would search	has searched
We	search – are searching	were searching	searched	will search	would search	have searched
You (pl)	search – are searching	were searching	searched	will search	would search	have searched
They	search – are searching	were searching	searched	will search	would search	have searched

The whole house was searched from top to bottom.

Are you searching for a flashlight?

Marie was searching for Pete in the underground tunnel.

to leave

to be left

leave!

Sub.	Present Simple Present Cont.	Past Continuous	Past Simple	Future	Conditional	Present Perfect
I	leave – am leaving	was leaving	left	will leave	would leave	have left
You	leave – are leaving	were leaving	left	will leave	would leave	have left
He She It	leaves – is leaving	was leaving	left	will leave	would leave	has left
We	leave – are leaving	were leaving	left	will leave	would leave	have left
You (pl)	leave – are leaving	were leaving	left	will leave	would leave	have left
They	leave – are leaving	were leaving	left	will leave	would leave	have left

Finally, Pete **left** the drain through the manhole.

Marie, I'**ll** never **leave** you!

Leave it alone, Pete! You're just emotional. (= *Stop talking like that! idiomatic*)

28

Sub.	Present Simple Present Cont.	Past Continuous	Past Simple	Future	Conditional	Present Perfect
I	shower – am showering	was showering	showered	will shower	would shower	have showered
You	shower – are showering	were showering	showered	will shower	would shower	have showered
He She It	showers – is showering	was showering	showered	will shower	would shower	has showered
We	shower – are showering	were showering	showered	will shower	would shower	have showered
You (pl)	shower – are showering	were showering	showered	will shower	would shower	have showered
They	shower – are showering	were showering	showered	will shower	would shower	have showered

Marie **showers** every morning for twenty minutes.

Were you **showering** when I called yesterday?

Today, Marie was showered with praise by Pete for her help. (= *Pete praised Marie profusely. idiomatic*)

29

to be combed

comb!

Sub.	Present Simple Present Cont.	Past Continuous	Past Simple	Future	Conditional	Present Perfect
I	comb – am combing	was combing	combed	will comb	would comb	have combed
You	comb – are combing	were combing	combed	will comb	would comb	have combed
He She It	combs – is combing	was combing	combed	will comb	would comb	has combed
We	comb – are combing	were combing	combed	will comb	would comb	have combed
You (pl)	comb – are combing	were combing	combed	will comb	would comb	have combed
They	comb – are combing	were combing	combed	will comb	would comb	have combed

Marie **was combing** her long, red hair.

I **comb** my hair three times a day.

Pete **combed** through his papers until he found the party invitation. (= *Pete searched his papers thoroughly. idiomatic*)

getting dressed
get dressed!

to get dressed
to be got(ten) dressed

Sub.	Present Simple Present Cont.	Past Continuous	Past Simple	Future	Conditional	Present Perfect
I	get dressed am getting dressed	was getting dressed	got dressed	will get dressed	would get dressed	have got dressed
You	get dressed are getting dressed	were getting dressed	got dressed	will get dressed	would get dressed	have got dressed
He She It	gets dressed is getting dressed	was getting dressed	got dressed	will get dressed	would get dressed	has got dressed
We	get dressed are getting dressed	were getting dressed	got dressed	will get dressed	would get dressed	have got dressed
You (pl)	get dressed are getting dressed	were getting dressed	got dressed	will get dressed	would get dressed	have got dressed
They	get dressed are getting dressed	were getting dressed	got dressed	will get dressed	would get dressed	have got dressed

Marie and Pete **are getting dressed** to go to a party.

Getting dressed **takes me two minutes—it takes Marie thirty!**

Even Toby likes to get dressed **up. (= *To dress in smart clothes*)**

31

to arrive

no passive

Sub.	Present Simple Present Cont.	Past Continuous	Past Simple	Future	Conditional	Present Perfect
I	arrive — am arriving	was arriving	arrived	will arrive	would arrive	have arrived
You	arrive — are arriving	were arriving	arrived	will arrive	would arrive	have arrived
He She It	arrives — is arriving	was arriving	arrived	will arrive	would arrive	has arrived
We	arrive — are arriving	were arriving	arrived	will arrive	would arrive	have arrived
You (pl)	arrive — are arriving	were arriving	arrived	will arrive	would arrive	have arrived
They	arrive — are arriving	were arriving	arrived	will arrive	would arrive	have arrived

We **will arrive** on time, provided we don't get lost.

Have Pete and Marie **arrived** yet? I haven't seen them.

They finally **arrived** at nine o'clock.

32

Sub.	Present Simple Present Cont.	Past Continuous	Past Simple	Future	Conditional	Present Perfect
I	see — am seeing	was seeing	saw	will see	would see	have seen
You	see — are seeing	were seeing	saw	will see	would see	have seen
He She It	sees — is seeing	was seeing	saw	will see	would see	has seen
We	see — are seeing	were seeing	saw	will see	would see	have seen
You (pl)	see — are seeing	were seeing	saw	will see	would see	have seen
They	see — are seeing	were seeing	saw	will see	would see	have seen

Oh dear! What has Marie seen ?

She saw Pete flirting with the blonde.

I will see to it that Pete is sorry! (= *I will ensure that Pete is sorry!*)

to scream

to be screamed

Sub.	Present Simple Present Cont.	Past Continuous	Past Simple	Future	Conditional	Present Perfect
I	scream – am screaming	was screaming	screamed	will scream	would scream	have screamed
You	scream – are screaming	were screaming	screamed	will scream	would scream	have screamed
He She It	screams – is screaming	was screaming	screamed	will scream	would scream	has screamed
We	scream – are screaming	were screaming	screamed	will scream	would scream	have screamed
You (pl)	scream – are screaming	were screaming	screamed	will scream	would scream	have screamed
They	scream – are screaming	were screaming	screamed	will scream	would scream	have screamed

Marie screamed. She was very angry!

Would you scream in her situation?

I think she is screaming blue murder! (= *She is screaming very angrily. idiomatic*)

34

Sub.	Present Simple Present Cont.	Past Continuous	Past Simple	Future	Conditional	Present Perfect
I	hear – am hearing	was hearing	heard	will hear	would hear	have heard
You	hear – are hearing	were hearing	heard	will hear	would hear	have heard
He She It	hears – is hearing	was hearing	heard	will hear	would hear	has heard
We	hear – are hearing	were hearing	heard	will hear	would hear	have heard
You (pl)	hear – are hearing	were hearing	heard	will hear	would hear	have heard
They	hear – are hearing	were hearing	heard	will hear	would hear	have heard

Pete, dear, I think I hear a scream. Did you?

Yes, that scream was heard around the whole town!

Will Marie hear me out when I try to explain? (= *Will Marie listen to all my explanations, without interrupting or leaving?*)

35

Sub.	Present Simple / Present Cont.	Past Continuous	Past Simple	Future	Conditional	Present Perfect
I	fight / am fighting	was fighting	fought	will fight	would fight	have fought
You	fight / are fighting	were fighting	fought	will fight	would fight	have fought
He She It	fights / is fighting	was fighting	fought	will fight	would fight	has fought
We	fight / are fighting	were fighting	fought	will fight	would fight	have fought
You (pl)	fight / are fighting	were fighting	fought	will fight	would fight	have fought
They	fight / are fighting	were fighting	fought	will fight	would fight	have fought

Our heroes **were fighting** like cat and dog. (= *They were fighting very hard. idiomatic*)

A fierce battle was fought that evening!

They should be ashamed of their fighting each other!

Sub.	Present Simple Present Cont.	Past Continuous	Past Simple	Future	Conditional	Present Perfect
I	separate – am separating	was separating	separated	will separate	would separate	have separated
You	separate – are separating	were separating	separated	will separate	would separate	have separated
He She It	separates is separating	was separating	separated	will separate	would separate	has separated
We	separate – are separating	were separating	separated	will separate	would separate	have separated
You (pl)	separate – are separating	were separating	separated	will separate	would separate	have separated
They	separate – are separating	were separating	separated	will separate	would separate	have separated

Separate them or they'll kill each other!

The bouncer **has** finally **separated** Pete and Marie.

Behave, or I **will separate** your head from your body! (= *I will hurt you badly. figurative*)

37

to close
to be closed

Sub.	Present Simple Present Cont.	Past Continuous	Past Simple	Future	Conditional	Present Perfect
I	close – am closing	was closing	closed	will close	would close	have closed
You	close – are closing	were closing	closed	will close	would close	have closed
He She It	closes – is closing	was closing	closed	will close	would close	has closed
We	close – are closing	were closing	closed	will close	would close	have closed
You (pl)	close – are closing	were closing	closed	will close	would close	have closed
They	close – are closing	were closing	closed	will close	would close	have closed

Pete was standing in the doorway when Marie closed the door in his face.

I will not close my eyes to your flirting with pretty girls! (= *I will not ignore your flirting.*)

Fortunately for you, Pete, hotels never close!

38

to forget
to be forgotten

Sub.	Present Simple Present Cont.	Past Continuous	Past Simple	Future	Conditional	Present Perfect
I	forget am forgetting	was forgetting	forgot	will forget	woild forget	have forgotten
You	forget are forgetting	were forgetting	forgot	will forget	woild forget	have forgotten
He She It	forgets is forgetting	was forgetting	forgot	will forget	woild forget	has forgotten
We	forget are forgetting	were forgetting	forgot	will forget	woild forget	have forgotten
You (pl)	forget are forgetting	were forgetting	forgot	will forget	woild forget	have forgotten
They	forget are forgetting	were forgetting	forgot	will forget	woild forget	have forgotten

It seems that Pete's difficulties were soon forgotten.

Pete, have you forgotten the cause of your problems?

He would forget his head, if it weren't screwed on! (= *He is very forgetful. idiomatic*)

39

to remember

to be remembered

Sub.	Present Simple Present Cont.	Past Continuous	Past Simple	Future	Conditional	Present Perfect
I	remember am remembering	was remembering	remembered	will remember	would remember	have remembered
You	remember are remembering	were remembering	remembered	will remember	would remember	have remembered
He She It	remembers is remembering	was remembering	remembered	will remember	would remember	has remembered
We	remember are remembering	were remembering	remembered	will remember	would remember	have remembered
You (pl)	remember are remembering	were remembering	remembered	will remember	would remember	have remembered
They	remember are remembering	were remembering	remembered	will remember	would remember	have remembered

I don't think he wants to remember what happened.

Suddenly Pete remembered what he had done.

I remember Marie as a fun-loving girl! (= *I remember that Marie is a fun-loving type of person.*)

40

Sub.	Present Simple Present Cont.	Past Continuous	Past Simple	Future	Conditional	Present Perfect
It	rains − is raining	was raining	rained	will rain	would rain	has rained

It **was raining** as Marie and Toby sat on the beach.

Marie thought sadly, It's **raining** in my heart! (= *Marie is very sorrowful. figurative*)

And it **will rain** (on) Friday and Saturday, too.

to talk
to be talked

talking

talk!

Sub.	Present Simple Present Cont.	Past Continuous	Past Simple	Future	Conditional	Present Perfect
I	talk – am talking	was talking	talked	will talk	would talk	have talked
You	talk – are talking	were talking	talked	will talk	would talk	have talked
He She It	talks – is talking	was talking	talked	will talk	would talk	has talked
We	talk – are talking	were talking	talked	will talk	would talk	have talked
You (pl)	talk – are talking	were talking	talked	will talk	would talk	have talked
They	talk – are talking	were talking	talked	will talk	would talk	have talked

We need **to talk** through our disagreement, Marie! (= *We need to resolve our disagreement by talking.*)

Pete and Marie **are talking** in English, of course!

They **talked** until the cows came home. (= *They talked for a long time. idiomatic*)

Sub.	Present Simple Present Cont.	Past Continuous	Past Simple	Future	Conditional	Present Perfect
I	trip – am tripping	was tripping	tripped	will trip	would trip	have tripped
You	trip – are tripping	were tripping	tripped	will trip	would trip	have tripped
He She It	trips – is tripping	was tripping	tripped	will trip	would trip	has tripped
We	trip – are tripping	were tripping	tripped	will trip	would trip	have tripped
You (pl)	trip – are tripping	were tripping	tripped	will trip	would trip	have tripped
They	trip – are tripping	were tripping	tripped	will trip	would trip	have tripped

Watch out, Pete, or you **will trip**!

When you don't look where you are going, you **trip** over. (= *You trip and fall.*)

You **have** been **tripped** up by pretty girls! (= *Pretty girls have made you behave the wrong way. idiomatic*)

to kick
to be kicked

Sub.	Present Simple Present Cont.	Past Continuous	Past Simple	Future	Conditional	Present Perfect
I	kick – am kicking	was kicking	kicked	will kick	would kick	have kicked
You	kick – are kicking	were kicking	kicked	will kick	would kick	have kicked
He She It	kicks – is kicking	was kicking	kicked	will kick	would kick	has kicked
We	kick – are kicking	were kicking	kicked	will kick	would kick	have kicked
You (pl)	kick – are kicking	were kicking	kicked	will kick	would kick	have kicked
They	kick – are kicking	were kicking	kicked	will kick	would kick	have kicked

Pete wanted **to kick** his bad habits. (= *To get rid of his bad habits; idiomatic*)

Unfortunately, he **kicked** a heavy stone!

He **was kicking** himself for being so stupid. (= *He was annoyed with himself.*
idiomatic)

44

Sub.	Present Simple Present Cont.	Past Continuous	Past Simple	Future	Conditional	Present Perfect
I	think – am thinking	was thinking	thought	will think	would think	have thought
You	think – are thinking	were thinking	thought	will think	would think	have thought
He She It	thinks – is thinking	was thinking	thought	will think	would think	has thought
We	think – are thinking	were thinking	thought	will think	would think	have thought
You (pl)	think – are thinking	were thinking	thought	will think	would think	have thought
They	think – are thinking	were thinking	thought	will think	would think	have thought

Pete is thinking about what to say.

"I have been such a fool!" he thought.

I need to think up a way to make Marie happy. (= *To think hard to develop a plan*)

45

to be
no passive

being
be!

Sub.	Present Simple Present Cont.	Past Continuous	Past Simple	Future	Conditional	Present Perfect
I	am — am being	was being	was	will be	would be	have been
You	are — are being	were being	were	will be	would be	have been
He She It	is — is being	was being	was	will be	would be	has been
We	are — are being	were being	were	will be	would be	have been
You (pl)	are — are being	were being	were	will be	would be	have been
They	are — are being	were being	were	will be	would be	have been

I **am** what I **am**—a man with many faults.

Pete **has been** very thoughtful.

It **will be** difficult to win Marie back.

Note: many forms are commonly contracted: **I'm** (I am), **you're** (you are), **he's** (he is), **she's** (she is), **it's** (it is), **we're** (we are), **they're** (they are).

46

deciding
decide!

to decide
to be decided

Sub.	Present Simple Present Cont.	Past Continuous	Past Simple	Future	Conditional	Present Perfect
I	decide – am deciding	was deciding	decided	will decide	would decide	have decided
You	decide – are deciding	were deciding	decided	will decide	would decide	have decided
He She It	decides – is deciding	was deciding	decided	will decide	would decide	has decided
We	decide – are deciding	were deciding	decided	will decide	would decide	have decided
You (pl)	decide – are deciding	were deciding	decided	will decide	would decide	have decided
They	decide – are deciding	were deciding	decided	will decide	would decide	have decided

Pete is deciding what to do.

I will decide by tossing a coin.

Pete, stop playing Hamlet and decide on something! (= *Make a choice*.)

to know
to be known

Sub.	Present Simple Present Cont.	Past Continuous	Past Simple	Future	Conditional	Present Perfect
I	know – x	was knowing	knew	will know	would know	have known
You	know – x	were knowing	knew	will know	would know	have known
He She It	knows – x	was knowing	knew	will know	would know	has known
We	know – x	were knowing	knew	will know	would know	have known
You (pl)	know – x	were knowing	knew	will know	would know	have known
They	know – x	were knowing	knew	will know	would know	have known

At last he **knew** what to do.

I **know** Marie, and I **know** what she'll like.

But, Pete, little is known about the workings of the human brain!

48

Sub.	Present Simple / Present Cont.	Past Continuous	Past Simple	Future	Conditional	Present Perfect
I	change – am changing	was changing	changed	will change	would change	have changed
You	change – are changing	were changing	changed	will change	would change	have changed
He She It	changes – is changing	was changing	changed	will change	would change	has changed
We	change – are changing	were changing	changed	will change	would change	have changed
You (pl)	change – are changing	were changing	changed	will change	would change	have changed
They	change – are changing	were changing	changed	will change	would change	have changed

This bank changes currency.

Have you changed all your savings?

All his savings were changed into money for college. (= *All his savings were converted*.)

to learn

to be learned or learnt

Sub.	Present Simple Present Cont.	Past Continuous	Past Simple	Future	Conditional	Present Perfect
I	learn – am learning	was learning	learned or learnt	will learn	would learn	have learned or have learnt
You	learn – are learning	were learning	learned or learnt	will learn	would learn	have learned or have learnt
He She It	learns – is learning	was learning	learned or learnt	will learn	would learn	has learned or has learnt
We	learn – are learning	were learning	learned or learnt	will learn	would learn	have learned or have learnt
You (pl)	learn – are learning	were learning	learned or learnt	will learn	would learn	have learned or have learnt
They	learn – are learning	were learning	learned or learnt	will learn	would learn	have learned or have learnt

What subject will be learned/learnt at school today?

We are learning how to solve problems.

We also learned about Einstein's brilliant theories. (= *We were informed about Einstein's theories.*)

50

Sub.	Present Simple Present Cont.	Past Continuous	Past Simple	Future	Conditional	Present Perfect
I	study – am studying	was studying	studied	will study	would study	have studied
You	study – are studying	were studying	studied	will study	would study	have studied
He She It	studies – is studying	was studying	studied	will study	would study	has studied
We	study – are studying	were studying	studied	will study	would study	have studied
You (pl)	study – are studying	were studying	studied	will study	would study	have studied
They	study – are studying	were studying	studied	will study	would study	have studied

Pete studies very hard.

Last term we studied advanced physics; this term we're studying quantum
mechanics.

Students, will you please study for the exams! (= *Prepare for the exams by studying!*)

to dream

to be dreamed or dreamt

Sub.	Present Simple Present Cont.	Past Continuous	Past Simple	Future	Conditional	Present Perfect
I	dream – am dreaming	was dreaming	dreamed or dreamt	will dream	would dream	have dreamed or have dreamt
You	dream – are dreaming	were dreaming	dreamed or dreamt	will dream	would dream	have dreamed or have dreamt
He She It	dreams – is dreaming	was dreaming	dreamed or dreamt	will dream	would dream	has dreamed or has dreamt
We	dream – are dreaming	were dreaming	dreamed or dreamt	will dream	would dream	have dreamed or have dreamt
You (pl)	dream – are dreaming	were dreaming	dreamed or dreamt	will dream	would dream	have dreamed or have dreamt
They	dream – are dreaming	were dreaming	dreamed or dreamt	will dream	would dream	have dreamed or have dreamt

Pete dreams every night.

Last night he dreamed/dreamt about dancing! (= *He had mental pictures of dancing.*)

You want to get back with Marie? Dream on! (= *You are deceiving yourself. idiomatic*)

52

Sub.	Present Simple Present Cont.	Past Continuous	Past Simple	Future	Conditional	Present Perfect
I	start – am starting	was starting	started	will start	would start	have started
You	start – are starting	were starting	started	will start	would start	have started
He She It	starts – is starting	was starting	started	will start	would start	has started
We	start – are starting	were starting	started	will start	would start	have started
You (pl)	start – are starting	were starting	started	will start	would start	have started
They	start – are starting	were starting	started	will start	would start	have started

The athletes **will start** the race very soon.

Pete, you **started** to run too soon!

I plan to start off at a fast pace. (= *I plan to begin the process.*)

to finish

to be finished

Sub.	Present Simple Present Cont.	Past Continuous	Past Simple	Future	Conditional	Present Perfect
I	finish — am finishing	was finishing	finished	will finish	would finish	have finished
You	finish — are finishing	were finishing	finished	will finish	would finish	have finished
He She It	finishes — is finishing	was finishing	finished	will finish	would finish	has finished
We	finish — are finishing	were finishing	finished	will finish	would finish	have finished
You (pl)	finish — are finishing	were finishing	finished	will finish	would finish	have finished
They	finish — are finishing	were finishing	finished	will finish	would finish	have finished

Have you **finished** running yet?

Finish the race as fast as you can!

In this race, reader, **would** you **finish** first, second, or third?

Sub.	Present Simple Present Cont.	Past Continuous	Past Simple	Future	Conditional	Present Perfect
I	win – am winning	was winning	won	will win	would win	have won
You	win – are winning	were winning	won	will win	would win	have won
He She It	wins – is winning	was winning	won	will win	would win	has won
We	win – are winning	were winning	won	will win	would win	have won
You (pl)	win – are winning	were winning	won	will win	would win	have won
They	win – are winning	were winning	won	will win	would win	have won

The race was won in one minute fifteen seconds.

Pete, you won first prize. Congratulations!

I will also win Marie's heart.

to (tell a) lie

no passive

lie!

Sub.	Present Simple Present Cont.	Past Continuous	Past Simple	Future	Conditional	Present Perfect
I	lie – am lying	was lying	lied	will lie	would lie	have lied
You	lie – are lying	were lying	lied	will lie	would lie	have lied
He She It	lies – is lying	was lying	lied	will lie	would lie	has lied
We	lie – are lying	were lying	lied	will lie	would lie	have lied
You (pl)	lie – are lying	were lying	lied	will lie	would lie	have lied
They	lie – are lying	were lying	lied	will lie	would lie	have lied

Pete **was lying** when he explained why he was late.

Are you **lying** to me about your car troubles? (= *Are you giving me false information on something?*)

"I don't like to lie," Pete **lied**.

56

testing
test!

to test
to be tested

Sub.	Present Simple Present Cont.	Past Continuous	Past Simple	Future	Conditional	Present Perfect
I	test — am testing	was testing	tested	will test	would test	have tested
You	test — are testing	were testing	tested	will test	would test	have tested
He She It	tests — is testing	was testing	tested	will test	would test	has tested
We	test — are testing	were testing	tested	will test	would test	have tested
You (pl)	test — are testing	were testing	tested	will test	would test	have tested
They	test — are testing	were testing	tested	will test	would test	have tested

Students, this exam **will test** you thoroughly.

You **are testing** my patience! Hurry up! (= *You are challenging my patience. idiomatic*)

All students were being tested for signs of intelligence. (= *All students were checked for the presence of intelligence.*)

to drive

to be driven

drive!

GƏRNICƏ

Sub.	Present Simple / Present Cont.	Past Continuous	Past Simple	Future	Conditional	Present Perfect
I	drive – am driving	was driving	drove	will drive	would drive	have driven
You	drive – are driving	were driving	drove	will drive	would drive	have driven
He She It	drives – is driving	was driving	drove	will drive	would drive	has driven
We	drive – are driving	were driving	drove	will drive	would drive	have driven
You (pl)	drive – are driving	were driving	drove	will drive	would drive	have driven
They	drive – are driving	were driving	drove	will drive	would drive	have driven

The teacher drove home in his old car.

When did he learn to drive?

His poor driving will drive his wife to despair! (= *Will force to extreme emotions or measures; idiomatic*)

58

Sub.	Present Simple Present Cont.	Past Continuous	Past Simple	Future	Conditional	Present Perfect
I	count – am counting	was counting	counted	will count	would count	have counted
You	count – are counting	were counting	counted	will count	would count	have counted
He She It	counts – is counting	was counting	counted	will count	would count	has counted
We	count – are counting	were counting	counted	will count	would count	have counted
You (pl)	count – are counting	were counting	counted	will count	would count	have counted
They	count – are counting	were counting	counted	will count	would count	have counted

Pete is counting from one to ten thousand.

Will he count up to one million?

I wouldn't count on it! (= *I wouldn't rely on that outcome.*)

to organize
to be organized

Sub.	Present Simple Present Cont.	Past Continuous	Past Simple	Future	Conditional	Present Perfect
I	organize – am organizing	was organizing	organized	will organize	would organize	have organized
You	organize – are organizing	were organizing	organized	will organize	would organize	have organized
He She It	organizes – is organizing	was organizing	organized	will organize	would organize	has organized
We	organize – are organizing	were organizing	organized	will organize	would organize	have organized
You (pl)	organize – are organizing	were organizing	organized	will organize	would organize	have organized
They	organize – are organizing	were organizing	organized	will organize	would organize	have organized

Pete has carefully organized his files.

Are the files organized alphabetically?

If you organize your things, you'll find them more easily.

Sub.	Present Simple Present Cont.	Past Continuous	Past Simple	Future	Conditional	Present Perfect
I	construct am constructing	was constructing	constructed	will construct	would construct	have constructed
You	construct are constructing	were constructing	constructed	will construct	would construct	have constructed
He She It	constructs is constructing	was constructing	constructed	will construct	would construct	has constructed
We	construct are constructing	were constructing	constructed	will construct	would construct	have constructed
You (pl)	construct are constructing	were constructing	constructed	will construct	would construct	have constructed
They	construct are constructing	were constructing	constructed	will construct	would construct	have constructed

Now Pete is constructing a machine.

I have constructed it with my own tools!

The machine was constructed out of scrap metal, recycled plastics, and junk.

to clean
to be cleaned

Sub.	Present Simple / Present Cont.	Past Continuous	Past Simple	Future	Conditional	Present Perfect
I	clean – am cleaning	was cleaning	cleaned	will clean	would clean	have cleaned
You	clean – are cleaning	were cleaning	cleaned	will clean	would clean	have cleaned
He She It	cleans – is cleaning	was cleaning	cleaned	will clean	would clean	has cleaned
We	clean – are cleaning	were cleaning	cleaned	will clean	would clean	have cleaned
You (pl)	clean – are cleaning	were cleaning	cleaned	will clean	would clean	have cleaned
They	clean – are cleaning	were cleaning	cleaned	will clean	would clean	have cleaned

Marie will be surprised that Pete has cleaned the machine.

He never even cleans his bedroom!

"Clean up after yourself!" she would shout. (= "Tidy the mess you make!")

62

Sub.	Present Simple Present Cont.	Past Continuous	Past Simple	Future	Conditional	Present Perfect
I	polish am polishing	was polishing	polished	will polish	would polish	have polished
You	polish are polishing	were polishing	polished	will polish	would polish	have polished
He She It	polishes is polishing	was polishing	polished	will polish	would polish	has polished
We	polish are polishing	were polishing	polished	will polish	would polish	have polished
You (pl)	polish are polishing	were polishing	polished	will polish	would polish	have polished
They	polish are polishing	were polishing	polished	will polish	would polish	have polished

Pete was polishing the machine when suddenly he saw his reflection.

Polishing is very hard work!

After all that work, he polished off a whole steak. (= *He ate an entire steak.*)

Sub.	Present Simple Present Cont.	Past Continuous	Past Simple	Future	Conditional	Present Perfect
I	write – am writing	was writing	wrote	will write	would write	have written
You	write – are writing	were writing	wrote	will write	would write	have written
He She It	writes – is writing	was writing	wrote	will write	would write	has written
We	write – are writing	were writing	wrote	will write	would write	have written
You (pl)	write – are writing	were writing	wrote	will write	would write	have written
They	write – are writing	were writing	wrote	will write	would write	have written

Meanwhile, Marie is writing to Pete.

I have written up a report on Pete's faults. (= *I have compiled a document.*)

Tomorrow I will write some e-mails.

Sub.	Present Simple Present Cont.	Past Continuous	Past Simple	Future	Conditional	Present Perfect
I	receive – am receiving	was receiving	received	will receive	would receive	have received
You	receive – are receiving	were receiving	received	will receive	would receive	have received
He She It	receives – is receiving	was receiving	received	will receive	would receive	has received
We	receive – are receiving	were receiving	received	will receive	would receive	have received
You (pl)	receive – are receiving	were receiving	received	will receive	would receive	have received
They	receive – are receiving	were receiving	received	will receive	would receive	have received

If you sign here, sir, you will receive this letter.

I wonder whether Pete received my message?

Don't worry, Marie! Your letter was safely received by Pete.

65

Sub.	Present Simple Present Cont.	Past Continuous	Past Simple	Future	Conditional	Present Perfect
I	give – am giving	was giving	gave	will give	would give	have given
You	give – are giving	were giving	gave	will give	would give	have given
He She It	gives – is giving	was giving	gave	will give	would give	has given
We	give – are giving	were giving	gave	will give	would give	have given
You (pl)	give – are giving	were giving	gave	will give	would give	have given
They	give – are giving	were giving	gave	will give	would give	have given

Pete **is giving** Marie some yellow flowers.

Reader, **would** you **give** such pathetic flowers to someone you loved?

It seems that Marie **will** not **give** in to Pete's charms. (= *Marie will not be won over by Pete's charms.*)

Sub.	Present Simple Present Cont.	Past Continuous	Past Simple	Future	Conditional	Present Perfect
I	show – am showing	was showing	showed	will show	would show	have shown/ showed
You	show – are showing	were showing	showed	will show	would show	have shown/ showed
He She It	shows – is showing	was showing	showed	will show	would show	has shown/ showed
We	show – are showing	were showing	showed	will show	would show	have shown/ showed
You (pl)	show – are showing	were showing	showed	will show	would show	have shown/ showed
They	show – are showing	were showing	showed	will show	would show	have shown/ showed

And now I **will show** you my invention!

Pete then **showed** Marie his amazing time machine.

Look! Even Toby **has shown** up, sitting in the driver's seat! (= *Toby has appeared on the scene.*)

67

to kiss

to be kissed

kiss!

Sub.	Present Simple Present Cont.	Past Continuous	Past Simple	Future	Conditional	Present Perfect
I	kiss – am kissing	was kissing	kissed	will kiss	would kiss	have kissed
You	kiss – are kissing	were kissing	kissed	will kiss	would kiss	have kissed
He She It	kisses – is kissing	was kissing	kissed	will kiss	would kiss	has kissed
We	kiss – are kissing	were kissing	kissed	will kiss	would kiss	have kissed
You (pl)	kiss – are kissing	were kissing	kissed	will kiss	would kiss	have kissed
They	kiss – are kissing	were kissing	kissed	will kiss	would kiss	have kissed

Marie has kissed Pete all over his face.

I love to be kissed! Please don't stop!

Wait! Are you kissing up to me? (= *Are you pleasing me to gain a favo(u)r or advantage?*)

68

buying
buy!

to buy
to be bought

Sub.	Present Simple Present Cont.	Past Continuous	Past Simple	Future	Conditional	Present Perfect
I	buy – am buying	was buying	bought	will buy	would buy	have bought
You	buy – are buying	were buying	bought	will buy	would buy	have bought
He She It	buys – is buying	was buying	bought	will buy	would buy	has bought
We	buy – are buying	were buying	bought	will buy	would buy	have bought
You (pl)	buy – are buying	were buying	bought	will buy	would buy	have bought
They	buy – are buying	were buying	bought	will buy	would buy	have bought

Yes! There are new clothes to be bought—and Pete must help!

We're buying things for our trip.

Marie, you have bought up the entire department store! (= *You have purchased the entire stock.*)

69

to pay
to be paid

Sub.	Present Simple Present Cont.	Past Continuous	Past Simple	Future	Conditional	Present Perfect
I	pay – am paying	was paying	paid	will pay	would pay	have paid
You	pay – are paying	were paying	paid	will pay	would pay	have paid
He She It	pays – is paying	was paying	paid	will pay	would pay	has paid
We	pay – are paying	were paying	paid	will pay	would pay	have paid
You (pl)	pay – are paying	were paying	paid	will pay	would pay	have paid
They	pay – are paying	were paying	paid	will pay	would pay	have paid

At the supermarket, Marie paid for her shopping. (= *Marie bought the items she had shopped for.*)

Are you paying by credit card or cash?

Fortunately I was paid today. My job pays me once every two weeks.

70

Sub.	Present Simple Present Cont.	Past Continuous	Past Simple	Future	Conditional	Present Perfect
I	go – am going	was going	went	will go	would go	have been
You	go – are going	were going	went	will go	would go	have been
He She It	goes – is going	was going	went	will go	would go	has been
We	go – are going	were going	went	will go	would go	have been
You (pl)	go – are going	were going	went	will go	would go	have been
They	go – are going	were going	went	will go	would go	have been

Now I'm **going** to take you for a flight in the time machine.

Let's **go** to the future, Pete! But don't **go** over the top! (= *Don't go to excess, i.e., too far into the future. idiomatic*)

So they **went** through the time barrier to the year 2080.

71

to get married
to be got(ten) married

get married!

Sub.	Present Simple Present Cont.	Past Continuous	Past Simple	Future	Conditional	Present Perfect
I	get married am getting married	was getting married	got married	will get married	would get married	have got married
You	get married are getting married	were getting married	got married	will get married	would get married	have got married
He She It	gets married is getting married	was getting married	got married	will get married	would get married	has got married
We	get married are getting married	were getting married	got married	will get married	would get married	have got married
You (pl)	get married are getting married	were getting married	got married	will get married	would get married	have got married
They	get married are getting married	were getting married	got married	will get married	would get married	have got married

Silence, please! Pete and Marie are getting married.

That's so cool! We just got married in the year 2080!

Would you get married by a pay-machine? (= *Would you have a pay-machine conduct your wedding?*)

72

Sub.	Present Simple Present Cont.	Past Continuous	Past Simple	Future	Conditional	Present Perfect
I	forbid am forbidding	was forbidding	forbade	will forbid	would forbid	have forbidden
You	forbid are forbidding	were forbidding	forbade	will forbid	would forbid	have forbidden
He She It	forbids is forbidding	was forbidding	forbade	will forbid	would forbid	has forbidden
We	forbid are forbidding	were forbidding	forbade	will forbid	would forbid	have forbidden
You (pl)	forbid are forbidding	were forbidding	forbade	will forbid	would forbid	have forbidden
They	forbid are forbidding	were forbidding	forbade	will forbid	would forbid	have forbidden

The authorities **have forbidden** swimming and jogging.

Smoking, taking photos, and dogs are also forbidden.

Madam, I **forbid** you to cut down that sign!

73

to swim

to be swum

swimming

swim!

garnica

Sub.	Present Simple Present Cont.	Past Continuous	Past Simple	Future	Conditional	Present Perfect
I	swim – am swimming	was swimming	swam	will swim	would swim	have swum
You	swim – are swimming	were swimming	swam	will swim	would swim	have swum
He She It	swims – is swimming	was swimming	swam	will swim	would swim	has swum
We	swim – are swimming	were swimming	swam	will swim	would swim	have swum
You (pl)	swim – are swimming	were swimming	swam	will swim	would swim	have swum
They	swim – are swimming	were swimming	swam	will swim	would swim	have swum

Pete **was swimming** in the sea, when a school of dolphins **swam** up. (= *When dolphins arrived by swimming*)

Pete **swims** the breaststroke and crawl; he can't do the butterfly.

Do you prefer to swim in the sea or in a pool?

74

Sub.	Present Simple / Present Cont.	Past Continuous	Past Simple	Future	Conditional	Present Perfect
I	love – am loving	was loving	loved	will love	would love	have loved
You	love – are loving	were loving	loved	will love	would love	have loved
He She It	loves – is loving	was loving	loved	will love	would love	has loved
We	love – are loving	were loving	loved	will love	would love	have loved
You (pl)	love – are loving	were loving	loved	will love	would love	have loved
They	love – are loving	were loving	loved	will love	would love	have loved

Pete **loves** Marie, and he **loves** the seaside.

I **have** always **loved** you, Marie!

I **would love** to dwell on this blissful scene, but we have twenty-six more verbs to go!

to jump

to be jumped

jumping

jump!

Sub.	Present Simple Present Cont.	Past Continuous	Past Simple	Future	Conditional	Present Perfect
I	jump – am jumping	was jumping	jumped	will jump	would jump	have jumped
You	jump – are jumping	were jumping	jumped	will jump	would jump	have jumped
He She It	jumps – is jumping	was jumping	jumped	will jump	would jump	has jumped
We	jump – are jumping	were jumping	jumped	will jump	would jump	have jumped
You (pl)	jump – are jumping	were jumping	jumped	will jump	would jump	have jumped
They	jump – are jumping	were jumping	jumped	will jump	would jump	have jumped

I think that Pete **is jumping** for joy.

No he isn't! Don't jump to conclusions. (= *Don't make assumptions! idiomatic*)

I know for a fact that he **jumps** rope for exercise.

76

Sub.	Present Simple Present Cont.	Past Continuous	Past Simple	Future	Conditional	Present Perfect
I	turn – am turning	was turning	turned	will turn	would turn	have turned
You	turn – are turning	were turning	turned	will turn	would turn	have turned
He She It	turns – is turning	was turning	turned	will turn	would turn	has turned
We	turn – are turning	were turning	turned	will turn	would turn	have turned
You (pl)	turn – are turning	were turning	turned	will turn	would turn	have turned
They	turn – are turning	were turning	turned	will turn	would turn	have turned

Pete's exercise **has turned** into a farce: his rope has become tangled on Marie's stick.

(= *Pete's exercise has transformed into a farce.*)

Marie was whistling as she **turned** the stick.

Marie, stop turning! I feel sick!

77

to watch
to be watched

watching
watch!

Sub.	Present Simple Present Cont.	Past Continuous	Past Simple	Future	Conditional	Present Perfect
I	watch – am watching	was watching	watched	will watch	would watch	have watched
You	watch – are watching	were watching	watched	will watch	would watch	have watched
He She It	watches – is watching	was watching	watched	will watch	would watch	has watched
We	watch – are watching	were watching	watched	will watch	would watch	have watched
You (pl)	watch – are watching	were watching	watched	will watch	would watch	have watched
They	watch – are watching	were watching	watched	will watch	would watch	have watched

These blasted cameras are watching us everywhere!

Pete, watch your language! (= *Stop using bad language! idiomatic*)

I like watching TV, but I don't like to be watched. Let's go home!

Sub.	Present Simple Present Cont.	Past Continuous	Past Simple	Future	Conditional	Present Perfect
I	return – am returning	was returning	returned	will return	would return	have returned
You	return – are returning	were returning	returned	will return	would return	have returned
He She It	returns – is returning	was returning	returned	will return	would return	has returned
We	return – are returning	were returning	returned	will return	would return	have returned
You (pl)	return – are returning	were returning	returned	will return	would return	have returned
They	return – are returning	were returning	returned	will return	would return	have returned

Our heroes **are returning** to the present with a bump.

It's great to be back! We **will** not **return** to 2080 any time soon!

Pete, **have** you **returned** your books on time travel to the library?

79

to walk

to be walked

walk!

Sub.	Present Simple Present Cont.	Past Continuous	Past Simple	Future	Conditional	Present Perfect
I	walk — am walking	was walking	walked	will walk	would walk	have walked
You	walk — are walking	were walking	walked	will walk	would walk	have walked
He She It	walks — is walking	was walking	walked	will walk	would walk	has walked
We	walk — are walking	were walking	walked	will walk	would walk	have walked
You (pl)	walk — are walking	were walking	walked	will walk	would walk	have walked
They	walk — are walking	were walking	walked	will walk	would walk	have walked

Marie **is walking** into town.

I am used to walking in high heels.

If you want to know how, I **will walk** you through it. (= *I will explain how to do something step by step.*)

80

Sub.	Present Simple Present Cont.	Past Continuous	Past Simple	Future	Conditional	Present Perfect
I	ask (for) – am asking (for)	was asking (for)	asked (for)	will ask (for)	would ask (for)	have asked (for)
You	ask (for) – are asking (for)	were asking (for)	asked (for)	will ask (for)	would ask (for)	have asked (for)
He She It	asks (for) – is asking (for)	was asking (for)	asked (for)	will ask (for)	would ask (for)	has asked (for)
We	ask (for) – are asking (for)	were asking (for)	asked (for)	will ask (for)	would ask (for)	have asked (for)
You (pl)	ask (for) – are asking (for)	were asking (for)	asked (for)	will ask (for)	would ask (for)	have asked (for)
They	ask (for) – are asking (for)	were asking (for)	asked (for)	will ask (for)	would ask (for)	have asked (for)

Poor Max! All that card playing **was asking** for trouble. (= *Card playing was inviting misfortune.*)

Max **asked** Pete for some money for a burger.

Now he **is asking** the waiter for a five-course meal!

81

to enter

to be entered

Sub.	Present Simple Present Cont.	Past Continuous	Past Simple	Future	Conditional	Present Perfect
I	enter – am entering	was entering	entered	will enter	would enter	have entered
You	enter – are entering	were entering	entered	will enter	would enter	have entered
He She It	enters – is entering	was entering	entered	will enter	would enter	has entered
We	enter – are entering	were entering	entered	will enter	would enter	have entered
You (pl)	enter – are entering	were entering	entered	will enter	would enter	have entered
They	enter – are entering	were entering	entered	will enter	would enter	have entered

Meanwhile, Pete and Marie's house was being entered by Nico!

He entered through the window, stole some valuables, and then left.

The law says that breaking and entering is a crime.

Sub.	Present Simple Present Cont.	Past Continuous	Past Simple	Future	Conditional	Present Perfect
I	call – am calling	was calling	called	will call	would call	have called
You	call – are calling	were calling	called	will call	would call	have called
He She It	calls – is calling	was calling	called	will call	would call	has called
We	call – are calling	were calling	called	will call	would call	have called
You (pl)	call – are calling	were calling	called	will call	would call	have called
They	call – are calling	were calling	called	will call	would call	have called

Marie immediately called the police on her cell (mobile) phone.

Now Pete is calling his dog. As you know, his dog is called Toby.

This situation calls for your help, Toby! (= *This situation requires your help.*)

Saznica

Sub.	Present Simple Present Cont.	Past Continuous	Past Simple	Future	Conditional	Present Perfect
I	come – am coming	was coming	came	will come	would come	have come
You	come – are coming	were coming	came	will come	would come	have come
He She It	comes – is coming	was coming	came	will come	would come	has come
We	come – are coming	were coming	came	will come	would come	have come
You (pl)	come – are coming	were coming	came	will come	would come	have come
They	come – are coming	were coming	came	will come	would come	have come

Pete **has come** up with a great idea. (= *Has thought of*)

Come here, Toby! Smell the house for clues!

Fortunately Toby **came** across the thief's scent. (= *Discovered*)

Sub.	Present Simple Present Cont.	Past Continuous	Past Simple	Future	Conditional	Present Perfect
I	follow am following	was following	followed	will follow	would follow	have followed
You	follow are following	were following	followed	will follow	would follow	have followed
He She It	follows is following	was following	followed	will follow	would follow	has followed
We	follow are following	were following	followed	will follow	would follow	have followed
You (pl)	follow are following	were following	followed	will follow	would follow	have followed
They	follow are following	were following	followed	will follow	would follow	have followed

The police officers **were** soon **following** the footprints.

My father was a detective, you know. I'**m following** in his footsteps. (= *I have the same job as my father. idiomatic*)

Have you noticed? This page **follows** verb number 84 (*to come*).

Sub.	Present Simple Present Cont.	Past Continuous	Past Simple	Future	Conditional	Present Perfect
I	arrest – am arresting	was arresting	arrested	will arrest	would arrest	have arrested
You	arrest – are arresting	were arresting	arrested	will arrest	would arrest	have arrested
He She It	arrests – is arresting	was arresting	arrested	will arrest	would arrest	has arrested
We	arrest – are arresting	were arresting	arrested	will arrest	would arrest	have arrested
You (pl)	arrest – are arresting	were arresting	arrested	will arrest	would arrest	have arrested
They	arrest – are arresting	were arresting	arrested	will arrest	would arrest	have arrested

At last they arrested Nico.

We are arresting you for robbery. (= *Arrest for the crime of*)

How humiliating—to be arrested by these clowns!

86

Sub.	Present Simple Present Cont.	Past Continuous	Past Simple	Future	Conditional	Present Perfect
I	wait – am waiting	was waiting	waited	will wait	would wait	have waited
You	wait – are waiting	were waiting	waited	will wait	would wait	have waited
He She It	waits – is waiting	was waiting	waited	will wait	would wait	has waited
We	wait – are waiting	were waiting	waited	will wait	would wait	have waited
You (pl)	wait – are waiting	were waiting	waited	will wait	would wait	have waited
They	wait – are waiting	were waiting	waited	will wait	would wait	have waited

Nico is waiting for his freedom from jail.

I used to wait on tables; I'm still waiting . . . for my release.

Wait a minute! Does that mean Nico is still a "waiter"?

to wave

to be waved

Sub.	Present Simple / Present Cont.	Past Continuous	Past Simple	Future	Conditional	Present Perfect
I	wave – am waving	was waving	waved	will wave	would wave	have waved
You	wave – are waving	were waving	waved	will wave	would wave	have waved
He She It	waves – is waving	was waving	waved	will wave	would wave	has waved
We	wave – are waving	were waving	waved	will wave	would wave	have waved
You (pl)	wave – are waving	were waving	waved	will wave	would wave	have waved
They	wave – are waving	were waving	waved	will wave	would wave	have waved

Pete and Marie **waved** good-bye to their friends.

We **will wave** hello to you when we return.

The flag on the time machine **was waving** in the wind.

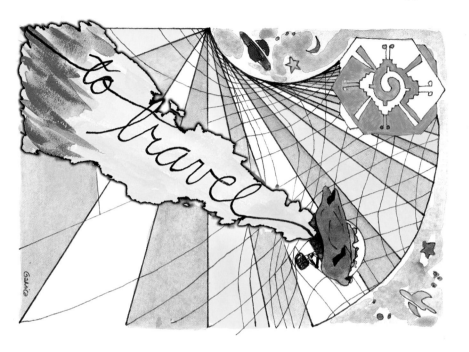

Sub.	Present Simple Present Cont.	Past Continuous	Past Simple	Future	Conditional	Present Perfect
I	travel – am travel(l)ing	was travel(l)ing	travel(l)ed	will travel	would travel	have travel(l)ed
You	travel – are travel(l)ing	were travel(l)ing	travel(l)ed	will travel	would travel	have travel(l)ed
He She It	travels – is travel(l)ing	was travel(l)ing	travel(l)ed	will travel	would travel	has travel(l)ed
We	travel – are travel(l)ing	were travel(l)ing	travel(l)ed	will travel	would travel	have travel(l)ed
You (pl)	travel – are travel(l)ing	were travel(l)ing	travel(l)ed	will travel	would travel	have travel(l)ed
They	travel – are travel(l)ing	were travel(l)ing	travel(l)ed	will travel	would travel	have travel(l)ed

Are they travel(l)ing to the future? No, to the past!

Pete, will we travel way back in time?

Let's travel around the solar system first! (= *Let's explore!*)

to crash
to be crashed

crash!

Sub.	Present Simple Present Cont.	Past Continuous	Past Simple	Future	Conditional	Present Perfect
I	crash – am crashing	was crashing	crashed	will crash	would crash	have crashed
You	crash – are crashing	were crashing	crashed	will crash	would crash	have crashed
He She It	crashes – is crashing	was crashing	crashed	will crash	would crash	has crashed
We	crash – are crashing	were crashing	crashed	will crash	would crash	have crashed
You (pl)	crash – are crashing	were crashing	crashed	will crash	would crash	have crashed
They	crash – are crashing	were crashing	crashed	will crash	would crash	have crashed

After a long flight, the time machine **crashed** into a field.

I think we **have crashed** a stone-age party! (= *We have turned up uninvited at a party.
idiomatic*)

Pete, you **crash** everything you drive! You always have accidents.

90

Sub.	Present Simple Present Cont.	Past Continuous	Past Simple	Future	Conditional	Present Perfect
I	repair – am repairing	was repairing	repaired	will repair	would repair	have repaired
You	repair – are repairing	were repairing	repaired	will repair	would repair	have repaired
He She It	repairs – is repairing	was repairing	repaired	will repair	would repair	has repaired
We	repair – are repairing	were repairing	repaired	will repair	would repair	have repaired
You (pl)	repair – are repairing	were repairing	repaired	will repair	would repair	have repaired
They	repair – are repairing	were repairing	repaired	will repair	would repair	have repaired

Pete, please repair our vehicle! I don't want to be stuck here forever.

No problem! I used to repair trains and buses.

Fortunately, the time machine was repaired in no time.

to be quiet

to be quieted

GaRNICE

Sub.	Present Simple Present Cont.	Past Continuous	Past Simple	Future	Conditional	Present Perfect
I	am quiet – am being quiet	was being quiet	was quiet	will be quiet	would be quiet	have been quiet
You	are quiet – are being quiet	were being quiet	were quiet	will be quiet	would be quiet	have been quiet
He She It	is quiet – is being quiet	was being quiet	was quiet	will be quiet	would be quiet	has been quiet
We	are quiet – are being quiet	were being quiet	were quiet	will be quiet	would be quiet	have been quiet
You (pl)	are quiet – are being quiet	were being quiet	were quiet	will be quiet	would be quiet	have been quiet
They	are quiet – are being quiet	were being quiet	were quiet	will be quiet	would be quiet	have been quiet

Shh, be quiet, Toby! And don't move!

If we are quiet, the animal will go away.

They were being very quiet as the mammoth examined the vehicle.

Sub.	Present Simple Present Cont.	Past Continuous	Past Simple	Future	Conditional	Present Perfect
I	light – am lighting	was lighting	lit	will light	would light	have lit
You	light – are lighting	were lighting	lit	will light	would light	have lit
He She It	lights – is lighting	was lighting	lit	will light	would light	has lit
We	light – are lighting	were lighting	lit	will light	would light	have lit
You (pl)	light – are lighting	were lighting	lit	will light	would light	have lit
They	light – are lighting	were lighting	lit	will light	would light	have lit

It is getting cold. I will light a fire.

If I had a box of matches, this fire would be lit easily.

Marie's face lit up when the fire began to blaze. (= *Marie's face brightened with pleasure*.)

93

to carry
to be carried

carrying
carry!

Sub.	Present Simple Present Cont.	Past Continuous	Past Simple	Future	Conditional	Present Perfect
I	carry — am carrying	was carrying	carried	will carry	would carry	have carried
You	carry — are carrying	were carrying	carried	will carry	would carry	have carried
He She It	carries — is carrying	was carrying	carried	will carry	would carry	has carried
We	carry — are carrying	were carrying	carried	will carry	would carry	have carried
You (pl)	carry — are carrying	were carrying	carried	will carry	would carry	have carried
They	carry — are carrying	were carrying	carried	will carry	would carry	have carried

Marie, help me to carry out a plan to advance mankind! (= *Help me to implement a plan.*)

So they carried some flintstones to the hut.

Cavepeople, these stones carry within the gift of fire!

Sub.	Present Simple Present Cont.	Past Continuous	Past Simple	Future	Conditional	Present Perfect
I	cut — am cutting	was cutting	cut	will cut	would cut	have cut
You	cut — are cutting	were cutting	cut	will cut	would cut	have cut
He She It	cuts — is cutting	was cutting	cut	will cut	would cut	has cut
We	cut — are cutting	were cutting	cut	will cut	would cut	have cut
You (pl)	cut — are cutting	were cutting	cut	will cut	would cut	have cut
They	cut — are cutting	were cutting	cut	will cut	would cut	have cut

We now **cut** to a page on crafts. (= *We suddenly change our focus [especially TV broadcasts, movies, etc.] to crafts.*)

I **will** now **cut** a pretty pattern.

Marie **has cut** the paper with scissors.

95

to make

to be made

making

make!

Sub.	Present Simple Present Cont.	Past Continuous	Past Simple	Future	Conditional	Present Perfect
I	make – am making	was making	made	will make	would make	have made
You	make – are making	were making	made	will make	would make	have made
He She It	makes – is making	was making	made	will make	would make	has made
We	make – are making	were making	made	will make	would make	have made
You (pl)	make – are making	were making	made	will make	would make	have made
They	make – are making	were making	made	will make	would make	have made

Meanwhile our time-travel(l)ers **have made** several stops.

Oh, Senator Pete, why **are** you **making** a sculpture?

Toga-clad Pete **was making** a dreadful noise!

recording
record!

to record
to be recorded

Sub.	Present Simple Present Cont.	Past Continuous	Past Simple	Future	Conditional	Present Perfect
I	record – am recording	was recording	recorded	will record	would record	have recorded
You	record – are recording	were recording	recorded	will record	would record	have recorded
He She It	records – is recording	was recording	recorded	will record	would record	has recorded
We	record – are recording	were recording	recorded	will record	would record	have recorded
You (pl)	record – are recording	were recording	recorded	will record	would record	have recorded
They	record – are recording	were recording	recorded	will record	would record	have recorded

This video records our visit to ancient Egypt.

The video camera was recording as Toby chased the camel.

These scenes have been recorded for posterity.

to eat
to be eaten

Sub.	Present Simple / Present Cont.	Past Continuous	Past Simple	Future	Conditional	Present Perfect
I	eat – am eating	was eating	ate	will eat	would eat	have eaten
You	eat – are eating	were eating	ate	will eat	would eat	have eaten
He She It	eats – is eating	was eating	ate	will eat	would eat	has eaten
We	eat – are eating	were eating	ate	will eat	would eat	have eaten
You (pl)	eat – are eating	were eating	ate	will eat	would eat	have eaten
They	eat – are eating	were eating	ate	will eat	would eat	have eaten

While Marie and Pete **were eating** snacks . . .

. . . the lion **ate** up a whole hunter!

We don't want **to be eaten**, so let's get out of here!

98

Sub.	Present Simple Present Cont.	Past Continuous	Past Simple	Future	Conditional	Present Perfect
I	stroll – am strolling	was strolling	strolled	will stroll	would stroll	have strolled
You	stroll – are strolling	were strolling	strolled	will stroll	would stroll	have strolled
He She It	strolls – is strolling	was strolling	strolled	will stroll	would stroll	has strolled
We	stroll – are strolling	were strolling	strolled	will stroll	would stroll	have strolled
You (pl)	stroll – are strolling	were strolling	strolled	will stroll	would stroll	have strolled
They	stroll – are strolling	were strolling	strolled	will stroll	would stroll	have strolled

Pete and Marie **are strolling** in the park.

While they **strolled** along, they met some weird people! (= *While wandering casually*)

Let's stroll over to the bandstand. (= *Let's wander in the direction of the bandstand.*)

99

to live

to be lived

living

live!

Sub.	Present Simple Present Cont.	Past Continuous	Past Simple	Future	Conditional	Present Perfect
I	live – am living	was living	lived	will live	would live	have lived
You	live – are living	were living	lived	will live	would live	have lived
He She It	lives – is living	was living	lived	will live	would live	has lived
We	live – are living	were living	lived	will live	would live	have lived
You (pl)	live – are living	were living	lived	will live	would live	have lived
They	live – are living	were living	lived	will live	would live	have lived

The world is our oyster. Where do you want to live?

Would you live in England, Canada, the United States, or somewhere else?

But, Pete, what will we live off? (= *What money or food will we survive on?*)

100

stopping
stop!

to stop
to be stopped

Sub.	Present Simple Present Cont.	Past Continuous	Past Simple	Future	Conditional	Present Perfect
I	stop – am stopping	was stopping	stopped	will stop	would stop	have stopped
You	stop – are stopping	were stopping	stopped	will stop	would stop	have stopped
He She It	stops – is stopping	was stopping	stopped	will stop	would stop	has stopped
We	stop – are stopping	were stopping	stopped	will stop	would stop	have stopped
You (pl)	stop – are stopping	were stopping	stopped	will stop	would stop	have stopped
They	stop – are stopping	were stopping	stopped	will stop	would stop	have stopped

Pete, why **are** you **stopping** the spaceship?

Do you want **to stop** off at your mother's house? (= *Do you want to drop by to see your mother?*)

No, that's not the reason. This verb, number 101, **has stopped** our story!

101

Verb Index

This index combines three features:

- All 101 conjugated verbs appear in **bold**, cross-referenced to their **page numbers**.
- Common phrasal verb forms of the 101 model verbs are listed under the main verb (followed by an explanation of each meaning in parentheses).
- An additional fifty common irregular verbs are included with their principal parts.

All irregular verbs are shown with following forms:

present simple • third person singular • present participle • past simple • past participle

The principal parts of regular verbs (**to** ———, ——— *(e)s*, ——— *ing*, ——— *(e)d*) are not shown.

to arise • arises • arising • arose • arisen
to arrest 86
to arrive 32
   to arrive at *(to reach a place or decision)*
to ask
   to ask about *(to inquire about)*
   to ask after *(to inquire about someone's well-being)*
   to ask for (to request) **81**
   to ask for it *(to deserve or provoke something negative happening)*
to be • is • being • was/were • been **46**
to be able (to) • is able to • being able to • was/were able to • been able to **4**
to be quiet • is quiet • being quiet • was/were quiet • been quiet **92**
to bear • bears • bearing • bore • borne
to beat • beats • beating • beat • beaten
to begin • begins • beginning • began • begun
to bite • bites • biting • bit • bitten
to blow • blows • blowing • blew • blown
to break • breaks • breaking • broke • broken
to bring • brings • bringing • brought • brought **12**
   to bring about *(to cause a particular outcome)*
   to bring on *(to encourage development)*
   to bring up *(to raise a subject for discussion)*
to build • builds • building • built • built
to buy • buys • buying • bought • bought **69**
   to buy into *(to buy partial ownership of; to accept an idea or proposal)*
   to buy out *(to purchase someone's entire stake in something)*
   to buy up *(to purchase a lot of)*
to call 83
   to call (a)round *(to telephone people in succession)*

to call by *(to visit)*
to call for *(to demand or request)*
to call off *(to cancel)*
to call on *(to visit; to request of someone)*
to call over *(to beckon to come here)*
to call up *(to telephone)*
can • can • ——— • could • ———
to carry 94
to carry off *(to take away; to accomplish)*
to carry out *(to implement a plan)*
to catch • catches • catching • caught • caught
to change 49
to change into *(to transform into; to change one's clothing for)*
to change over to *(to convert to)*
to choose • chooses • choosing • chose • chosen
to clean 62
to clean out *(to tidy by ridding of unwanted things)*
to clean up *(to tidy or to organize)*
to close 38
to close off *(to close entirely)*
to close up *(to shut)*
to comb 30
to come • comes • coming • came • come **84**
to come by *(to visit casually)*
to come into *(to enter; to gain, such as with inheritance money)*
to come off *(to detach; to happen successfully)*
to come on *(to hurry; to start working)*
to come over *(to appear to others; to visit)*
to come through *(to survive; to endure)*
to come to *(to add up to; to make of oneself; to reach)*
to construct 61
to cook 13
to cook up *(to prepare an amount of food; to invent an idea or plan)*
to cost • costs • costing • cost/costed • cost
to count 59
to count off *(to tally)*
to count up *(to add to a total)*
to crash 90
to crash into *(to collide with)*
to create 5
to cut • cuts • cutting • cut • cut **95**
to cut along *(to cut by following a line)*
to cut into *(to slice into)*
to cut off *(to detach by cutting)*
to cut through *(to slice through)*
to cut up *(to cut into pieces)*
to dance 7
to dance around *(to avoid an issue or problem)*
to decide 47
to decide for *(to make a decision in favo(u)r of)*
to decide on *(to make a decision about)*
to direct 1

to dig • digs • digging • dug • dug
to do • does • doing • did • done
to draw • draws • drawing • drew • drawn
to dream • dreams • dreaming • dreamed/dreamt • dreamed/dreamt   **52**
  to dream about *(to picture in one's sleep or fantasy)*
  to dream of *(to imagine; to conceive)*
  to dream up *(to invent)*
to drink • drinks • drinking • drank • drunk   **16**
  to drink up *(to drink all of)*
to drive • drives • driving • drove • driven   **58**
  to drive at *(to allude to; to suggest)*
to eat • eats • eating • ate • eaten   **98**
  to eat in *(to eat a meal at home)*
  to eat out *(to dine away from home)*
  to eat up *(to complete eating all of)*
  to overeat *(to eat to excess)*
to enter   **82**
  to enter into *(to take part in; to enrol[l])*
to fall • falls • falling • fell • fallen   **26**
  to fall for *(to develop romantic feelings toward)*
  to fall off *(to decline; to drop from something)*
  to fall through *(to fail [of a plan])*
  to fall (up)on *(to be dependent on; to encounter; to attack)*
to feed • feeds • feeding • fed • fed
to feel • feels • feeling • felt • felt
to fight • fights • fighting • fought • fought   **36**
  to fight over *(to battle with someone else for control or ownership of)*
  to fight through *(to successfully make one's way through a situation)*
to find • finds • finding • found • found   **10**
  to find out *(to discover)*
  to find out about *(to uncover the truth about)*
to finish   **54**
  to finish off *(to complete; to kill)*
  to finish up *(to conclude one's business)*
to fly • flies • flying • flew • flown
to follow   **85**
  to follow through *(to manage until a conclusion is reached)*
  to follow up *(to check on; to ensure something was done)*
to forbid • forbids • forbidding • forbade • forbidden   **73**
to forget • forgets • forgetting • forgot • forgotten   **39**
  to forget about *(to no longer remember something)*
to freeze • freezes • freezing • froze • frozen
to get • gets • getting • got/gotten • got/gotten
to get dressed • gets dressed • getting dressed • got(ten) dressed • got(ten) dressed   **31**
to get married • gets married • getting married • got(ten) married • got(ten) married   **72**
to give • gives • giving • gave given   **66**
  to give back *(to return; to surrender; to admit defeat)*
  to give out *(to distribute)*
  to give up *(to stop doing something in failure)*
to go • goes • going • went • gone   **71**
  to go along with *(to accept)*
  to go (a)round *(to circumnavigate; to reach one's aim by avoiding something)*

to go down *(to descend; to decrease; to decline)* **19**
to go out *(to exit; to extinguish [of a light, candle])*
to go through *(to proceed from one side to the other; to endure)*
to go under *(to fail financially)*
to go up *(to increase; to approach)*
to grow • grows • growing • grew • grown **11**
to grow into *(to develop into)*
to grow up *(to become more mature)*
to hang • hangs • hanging • hanged/hung • hanged/hung
to have • has • having • had • had **2**
to have against *(to bear a grudge against)*
to have around *(to invite to visit; to possess)*
to have on *(to be wearing)*
to hear • hears • hearing • heard • heard **35**
to hear about *(to learn about)*
to hear from *(to get a message from)*
to hear of *(to learn about the existence of)*
to hide • hides • hiding • hid • hidden
to hit • hits • hitting • hit • hit
to hold • holds • holding • held • held
to jump **76**
to jump down *(to leap in a downward motion)*
to jump in *(to decisively involve oneself in the situation)*
to jump over *(to leap over the top of)*
to jump up *(to leap upward[s]; to suddenly appear)*
to keep • keeps • keeping • kept • kept
to kick **44**
to kick off *(to start)*
to kick over *(to knock down)*
to kiss **68**
to kiss up *(to try to gain favo(u)r by praise)*
to kneel • kneels • kneeling • knelt/kneeled • knelt/kneeled
to know • knows • knowing • knew • known **48**
to know about *(to be aware of)*
to know of *(to be aware of the existence of)*
to leap • leaps • leaping • leapt/leaped • leapt/leaped
to learn • learns • learning • learned/learnt • learned/learnt **50**
to learn about *(to discover)*
to learn of *(to discover by chance)*
to learn through *(to find out by means of)*
to leave • leaves • leaving • left • left **28**
to lend • lends • lending • lent • lent
to let • lets • letting • let • let
to lie • lies • lying • lay • laid
to lie • lies • lying • lied • lied **56**
to lie about *(to tell an untruth about)*
to light • lights • lighting • lit • lit **93**
to light up *(to start to shine; to illuminate)*
to like **14**
to live **100**
to lose • loses • losing • lost • lost **23**
to lose out *(to end up at a disadvantage in a situation)*

to love 75
to make • makes • making • made • made **96**
   to make do *(to put up with; to settle for)*
   to make off with *(to steal; to go away with something)*
   to make up *(to invent)*
to mean • means • meaning • meant • meant
to meet • meets • meeting • met • met
to open 15
   to open up *(to open wide; to reveal one's thoughts or feelings)*
to organize 60
to paint 6
   to paint over *(to cover with paint)*
to pay • pays • paying • paid • paid **70**
   to pay in *(to put money into)*
   to pay off *(to settle an account; to pay what is owed)*
   to pay out *(to give winnings or earnings)*
to play 21
   to play along *(to pretend to follow)*
   to play around *(to act foolishly)*
   to play at *(to pretend to be)*
   to play on *(to continue playing; to exploit)*
   to play up *(to emphasize; to act erratically)*
   to play with *(to enjoy a game with; to toy with)*
to polish 63
   to polish off *(to completely finish; to eat entirely)*
to put • puts • putting • put • put **22**
   to put by *(to set aside)*
   to put off *(to postpone)*
to quit 9
to rain 41
   to rain down *(on) (to rain heavily; to occur in large numbers or amount)*
to read • reads • reading • read • read **8**
   to read between the lines *(to understand the hidden message)*
   to read over *(to look through)*
   to read through *(to read from start to finish)*
   to read up on *(to research)*
to receive 65
to record 97
to remember 40
to repair 91
to return 79
   to return for *(to come back to retrieve)*
   to return to *(to come back to)*
to ride • rides • riding • rode • ridden
to ring • rings • ringing • rang • rung
to rise • rises • rising • rose • risen
to run • runs • running • ran • run **25**
   to run around *(to be busy in activity)*
   to run by *(to briefly bring some information or idea to someone's notice for approval; to*
      stop by someplace quickly)
   to run into *(to meet by chance)*
   to run over *(to knock down)*

to say • says • saying • said • said
to scream 34
   to scream at *(to shout very loudly at)*
   to scream for *(to demand by yelling)*
to search 27
   to search for *(to look for)*
   to search out *(to seek and find)*
to see • sees • seeing • saw • seen **33**
   to see in *(to appreciate a quality)*
   to see off *(to successfully deter or reject; to accompany to departure)*
   to see through *(to be able to; to realize someone's real aim)*
to seem • seems • seeming • seemed • seemed
to sell • sells • selling • sold • sold
to send • sends • sending • sent • sent
to separate 37
to shine • shines • shining • shone • shone
to show • shows • showing • showed • shown **67**
   to show off *(to display ostentatiously)*
   to show through *(to be visible through something)*
   to show up *(to appear; to highlight failings)*
to shower 29
to sing • sings • singing • sang • sung **17**
to sit down • sits down • sitting down • sat down • sat down **20**
to sleep • sleeps • sleeping • slept • slept **18**
   to sleep over *(to stay the night at someone's house)*
   to sleep through *(to remain asleep for the duration)*
to spend • spends • sending • spent • spent
to spill • spills • spilling • spilled/spilt • spilled/spilt
to spin • spins • spinning • span • spun
to spit • spits • spitting • spat • spat
to stand • stands • standing • stood • stood
to start 53
   to start off *(to begin)*
   to start up *(to begin [especially, an engine, a company, a discussion])*
to steal • steals • stealing • stole • stolen
to stick • sticks • sticking • stuck • stuck
to stop 101
   to stop by *(to halt momentarily at)*
   to stop off at *(to halt one's journey at)*
   to stop up *(to clog)*
to stroll 99
   to stroll by *(to walk past)*
   to stroll into *(to walk casually into)*
to study 51
   to study under *(to be taught by a particular professor or other expert)*
to swim • swims • swimming • swam • swum **74**
to take • takes • taking • took • taken
to talk 42
   to talk about *(to discuss a subject)*
   to talk of *(to discuss)*
   to talk through *(to lead through by talking)*
   to talk up *(to exaggerate)*

to teach • teaches • teaching • taught • taught
to tear • tears • tearing • tore • torn
to tell • tells • telling • told • told
to (tell a) lie • tells a lie • telling a lie • told a lie • told a lie   **56**
to test   57
    to test for *(to conduct tests to determine the presence of something)*
to think • thinks • thinking • thought • thought   **45**
    to think of *(to come to mind)*
    to think through *(to mentally analyze the consequences)*
to throw • throws • throwing • threw • thrown
to travel   89
    to travel (a)round *(to journey to different places)*
to trip   43
    to trip over *(to stumble and fall)*
    to trip up *(to fall; to make a mistake; to make someone fail)*
to turn   77
    to turn (a)round *(to move in the opposite direction)*
    to turn off *(to switch off; to deter)*
    to turn on *(to switch on; to arouse)*
    to turn over *(to flip)*
    to turn up *(to appear)*
to understand • understands • understanding • understood • understood
to undo • undoes • undoing • undid • undone
to wait   87
    to wait on *(to attend to someone's needs)*
    to wait out *(to endure until the end)*
to wake • wakes • waking • woke • woken
to wake up • wakes up • waking up • woke up • woken up   **24**
to walk   80
    to walk away *(to depart; to avoid becoming involved in)*
    to walk off *(to leave the scene)*
    to walk over *(to treat badly)*
to want   3
    to want for *(to lack)*
to watch   78
    to watch out *(to keep alert to)*
to wave   88
to wear • wears • wearing • wore • worn
to win • wins • winning • won • won   **55**
    to win (a)round *(to persuade to one's point of view)*
    to win over *(to persuade to one's point of view)*
to write • writes • writing • wrote • written   **64**
    to write off *(to consider not worth saving)*
    to write up *(to write a report on)*